Strengthening Marital Intimacy

Strengthening Marital Intimacy

Ronald E. Hawkins

BAKER BOOK HOUSE
Grand Rapids, Michigan 49516

Library of Congress Cataloging-in-Publication Data

Hawkins, Ronald E.
    Strengthening marital intimacy / Ronald E. Hawkins.
    p. cm.
    ISBN 0-8010-4355-7
    1. Marriage—United States. 2. Intimacy (Psychology)
3. Marriage—Religious aspects—Christianity. I. Title.
    HQ734.H394 1991
    646.7'8—dc20   91-15373

To the one who is one with me
and yet wonderfully separate—with balance
Peg

I am deeply indebted to
Marie Chapman and Ruby Tyree
for assistance in editing this book.
Also, recognition is due my daughter Kim
and Kristy Musser
for typing the manuscript.

Contents

Preface

Marriage is a prison." "Marriage is not for me." "When you get married your life is over." How many times have you heard expressions like these? Currently many people have an extremely low view of marriage—a view not at all supported by the Scriptures.

Is there a reason for such a dark view? Yes, but I think the most significant contributing factor is a disregard for biblical teaching on how to build a strong marriage. We follow closely a recipe for our favorite pie, but when it comes to marriage, we throw in any ingredient and hope the pie turns out all right.

We need not flounder—following this advice or that—for there is a source of solid advice on how to build a strong marriage. As I have dealt with university students and have counseled couples for more than a decade, I have become convinced that great marriages do not happen by accident. "If you aim at nothing, you will hit it every time."

The answer to the question of "How can I build a strong marriage?" is found in God's Word. There, he gives his inerrant directions for the intimacy he intended. Through years of teaching and counseling, I have developed a framework for a model that can be summed up in two words, intimacy and commitment.

Intimacy is best defined as "oneness with healthy separateness." Occasionally, the female loses herself in her husband and becomes adrift in a sea of submission. While I believe in submission, I do not believe that either mate should ever lose his/her individual identity within the marriage experience. It is my con-

viction that two strong persons, covenantly committed to God
and each other, provide the substance for the kind of coupling
that will build strong marriages.

Commitment is a concept I lift high in this book. I seek here to
show the shallowness of today's society's commitment to self-
gratification. God-honoring marriages do not just happen. They
are the result of diligent prayer and hard work on the part of both
husband and wife. My purpose here is to provide couples with a
tool to help them strengthen their marriages.

Key concepts are intimacy, commitment, wisdom's directives,
reality, God's sovereignty, the person, sexuality, communication
and companionship. The book can be used as a supplement to
counseling, or it can be used independently by motivated couples.

I have attempted to write a book you can share, one that will
minister. It is my hope it will prove helpful to you.

Ronald E. Hawkins
Lynchburg, Va.

1

God's Design:
The Intimate Marriage

I love bumper stickers. I recently read two good ones. The first said: Don't follow me—I'm lost. The second said: Aim at nothing—you'll hit it every time.

Those nuggets describe well the way many couples regard marriage. I felt that way when I entered marriage twenty-seven years ago. I loved my wife dearly. However, I had no clear sense of where I wanted the marriage to go.

I came from a non-Christian home and had never seen a godly husband or father in action. Being a new Christian I was familiar with some Bible passages but knew no way to apply them to our marriage.

The usual trial-and-error process through the years has taught me much about marriage. Often I failed my wife, Peg. Frequently I have been a klutz. Our love for one another has been sorely tried but has never died. Our common commitment to Christ and to our love has brought us to the point of a truly intimate relationship.

This status has not been achieved by accident. As we understood biblical principles we committed ourselves to obey those directives. Even now, as great as our marriage has become, we could lose that intimacy, that oneness, if we were to stop walking as obedient children of God.

Small wonder so many marriages end in divorce. We, too, have frequently felt the pressures that contribute to tragic endings and have been tempted to quit. But, by God's grace, we have not given up on ourselves or each other. Our relationship has become stronger with the passing of time.

We have discovered many erroneous ideas about what intimacy in marriage is all about. Definitions of intimacy often suggest a mushy-mystical oneness that obliterates or subordinates one person. These definitions smack of a smothering overinvolvement in each other's lives that results in loss of individuality.

A better definition emphasizes the separateness of the individuals while it stresses their oneness. I define intimacy as oneness with healthy separateness. One personality should not dominate the other, for people tend to lose respect for what they dominate. Without respect they find it difficult to love, for these two relationship-enhancing concepts are closely related.

Achieving intimacy requires a commitment to oneness; therefore, the two persons must enter into covenant with each other. When a strong sense of separate self-worth unites with a strong commitment to a partner, then, and only then, is intimacy possible.

God created males and females in his image and designed them to complement each other. Each sex possesses unique strengths. Males and females are capable of far greater good together than they can achieve in isolation from one another. Culturally taught messages or customs that imply the superiority or inferiority of either sex are not supported by the Bible and do great harm to both men and women.

Since the entrance of sin into the human family, men and women are victims of a satanic wedge. This wedge has devastating consequences for their relationships. In Christ, through the power of the Holy Spirit, it is God's intent to remove the satanic wedge. In so doing, God desires to restore husbands and wives to a biblical sense of teamwork.

According to the United States Census Bureau, one half of all American couples who marry today will eventually divorce, and 55 percent of all second marriages will end in divorce. The divorce rate among evangelicals is fast catching up with the national average, even in the Bible Belt states. Adultery, which once was even (unscripturally) deemed "the unpardonable sin" by the church, is today often accepted as a way of life.

The Bible mandates a better way. Dr. Ed Wheat reminds us of this better way when he says, "In scripture, among all the other principles set forth, there is one basic, attitude-transforming truth related to marriage. God's will in every marriage is that the couple love each other with an absorbing spiritual, emotional and physical attraction that continues to grow throughout their lifetime together."

The Team: *God's Desire*

God created male and female to function as a team and share the joys of God's creation. Satan drove a wedge between them, and over the centuries males and females have been locked in a tragic power struggle. Christ came to restore people to fellowship with God, their Creator, and with each other. Christ is the wedge remover who restores the original intention of God.

In the realm of sports, whole schools are united in one common cause: the victory of their team. Husbands and wives who recognize they are on the same team, striving for the success of their marriage, make an unbeatable combination.

You may not be experiencing success as a marital team right now, but there is hope. You can rekindle your love. You can learn how to handle the most difficult problems in such a way that your marriage will become rooted in love and built on a firm foundation. Strong pillars can sustain that love in times of difficulty and stress. Even if you are trying to save your marriage by yourself (without cooperation from your spouse), it can happen. With God, nothing is impossible; all things are possible with him.

The following pages will present key biblical concepts that are basic for successful marital relationships and on which stronger

marriages can be constructed. These will benefit only those individuals and couples who put them into practice in the everyday
building of their marriages.

Matthew 7:24–27 records a familiar parable. Two men each
built a house. One Jesus called wise and the other foolish. What
made the difference? In verse 24 Jesus said, "Therefore, whosoever
heareth these sayings of mine, and doeth them, I will liken him
unto a wise man." In verse 26 he said, "And every one that
heareth these sayings of mine, and doeth them not, shall be
likened unto a foolish man." The whole emphasis is on doing.

Giving lip service to him did not suffice then, nor will mere
mental assent to the principles Jesus taught suffice now. Building
an intimate relationship requires doing. Building is done block by
block, step by step. Will you be wise or foolish? I don't think any-
body desires to be a fool. Let me challenge you, husband, and
you, wife, to work together to build an intimate marriage.

The First Marriage: *Adam and Eve*

It may be helpful to begin the process by taking a look at the
world's first marriage to discover God's intent for the marital
relationship. What can we say about this team? They were created in God's image (Gen. 1:26–28). Male and female were *both*
created in God's image. As a team, they were to exercise dominion
over the living things of the earth. Their relationship was not
governed by concerns over power or hierarchical issues of control.

They were created to function as a team. Male leadership was
based solely on the divine prerogative and methodology, not on
any implied superiority or inferiority of the sexes. God never
begins an institution without a chain of command. Consider the
church (Eph. 4:23), the home (Eph. 4:23, 24; 6:1–3), and the
mandate for social order (Titus 3:1).

Wives are referred to as helpmeets for their husbands in
Genesis 2:18. The term *helpmeet* comes from two Hebrew
words: *ezer* and *neged*. In our culture we tend to think of a
helper as someone who is an assistant, of lower status. In the
original language that is not the meaning; the woman is not
inferior in status.

Ezer, the word for "help" or "helper," occurs repeatedly in the Old Testament. It never refers to a subordinate helper. Note the reference to God as our helper in Psalm 121:1–2.

Neged means "corresponding to" or "fit for." The woman fits the man in a complementing fashion.

The combined sense of *ezer* and *neged* is that Eve was an appropriate, suitable partner for Adam. Rather than being proof of a subordinate position for Eve, these words support her position as Adam's complement. She was designed to be a *real* help. Woman was, like Adam, suitable in every way. Each brought to the team unique strengths and attributes without which humanity would have been impoverished and with which humanity was greatly enriched to serve as a fuller revelation of God's image.

Adam and Eve were created to complement each other in physiological procreation (Gen. 1:28) and psychological differences.

These differences as God designed them are complementary. Neither men nor women are superior. God so designed males and females so that all would fit together to create a functional and full humanity.

The couple forms a team. Humanity depends on the congenial and complementary relationship of man and woman. What a wonderful plan! The divine plan for humanity is like a triangle. Male and female are at the ends of the baseline with God at the apex. As males and females draw closer to the Creator they draw closer to each other. Chaos results from the abandonment of this divine plan.

The Satanic Wedge

Satan drove a wedge between male and female—sin. War and walls came into existence between men and women as a consequence of that wedge. Adam sought to rule his helpmeet with a calloused indifference for her needs and no appreciation for his desperate need of her enriching strengths. When Adam and Eve rebelled against the divine command, kindness fled from their relationship like dew fleeing before the rising sun. Her desire was now "for" her husband. The term *for* in the Hebrew means "against"—against the rule. She positioned herself as an antagonist ready to throw off his oppressive rule. The battle lines between the sexes were drawn.

Some use Genesis 3:16 to say that God decreed that the woman must be the follower and submitter and that the man should be the leader and authority. We must ask whether this information is a decree from God or a prediction. Is he saying that this is the way it must be, or that it is the way things will go as a natural consequence of their sin?

Considering the context, it is clear that all the references to the man, the soil, and death are predictions. The Hebrew construction is a form generally used in a predictive sense, and it is correct, therefore, for us to see this passage as predictive. God in effect said, "This is the way the world will go." As a result of the fall the man would rule despotically, and Eve's desire would be to overthrow Adam's unloving leadership. As a consequence of their disobedient choices, the struggle for power and control was now a central factor in this formerly peaceful team's relationship and in the relationship of all their offspring for millenniums to come.

The powerful of this world have continued to exploit, rule over, and mistreat the vulnerable. Husbands deny their wives what they want and need. They become the oppressors, and wives become the oppressed. Wives retaliate and strike back at such a sinful display of power. The human family descended from Adam and Eve illustrates a never ending cycle of exploitation and retaliation, that in its extreme leads to such dehumanizing acts as wife battering, divorce, violent sex crimes, and other tragic demonstrations of distorted male-female relationships. Hardly a newscast ends without one sex-oriented crime report. Many are not sudden "crimes of passion" but "the straw that broke the camel's back" in relationships destroyed by hatred and war.

The sad results of the Fall were not part of God's original design at all. When the team broke down, humanity through all its future millenniums of development became the loser. Wedges have appeared everywhere between males and females as they engaged in acts of belligerence toward one another and jockeyed for power.

The New Testament tells us there was a wall between the Jews and Greeks (Eph. 2:14). Paul tells us that Jesus Christ through the power of the cross broke down that wall. God can break down the walls that exist between males and females. In Christ the war can cease and the wedge can be removed. Males will still hold their places as leaders in their marriages by divine appointment. However, they will lead from love, not power, and all discussions related to the superiority or inferiority of persons based on gender or other considerations will disappear in the light of Christ's gracious lordship.

Christ, the Wedge Remover

Salvation restores fellowship with God. God provided a Savior to mend the broken relationships between fallen human beings and himself (Rom. 5:6–11).

When Bob and Sandra accepted Christ into their hearts and lives, both came under new management. This new management had a drastic impact on their relationship. Before Christ began to transform them, their marriage had been filled with one battle after another. Now they delight to serve one another; forgiving and serving are major themes in their marriage. Sandy says, "We now have an A.C. (after Christ) relationship." Daily the Holy Spirit teaches each of them lessons on submission. Both now seek to honor the God who made them.

Christ can and does heal broken relationships. In Christ, all become one, "neither Jew nor Greek . . . male nor female" (Gal. 3:26–29; Eph. 2:11–22). The Holy Spirit teaches Christians how to reunite themselves. The breaks can be mended (Eph. 5:18–33), wedges removed, and walls broken down. Janet set the pattern when she married Ted, a nominal Sunday-morning Christian. Noting her invariable kindness and consideration, Ted began to pick up the Bible that stayed on the coffee table, seeking answers to the question, What makes her different? He found her Lord. Together they seek to please him in their lives.

Freedom in Christ and the equality of believers can carry them on to provide equal opportunity in the marriage for the expression of each partner's full personhood. There is freedom in him (John

8:32). This freedom involves us in commitment to unity and the preservation of individuality (1 Cor. 12:1–31).

God wants to work through his creatures to reverse the bad effects of the Fall. It is time to work with him to reinstate the original relationship of perfect love between man and woman in marriage.

Conclusion

Christ is the wedge remover. His Holy Spirit, living in the believer, breaks down walls that divide. As you trust him and take practical steps to comply with biblical principles, the wedge between you and your spouse can be removed. Perhaps you consider your marriage to be a good one. Yet you, too, can glean truths and principles from God's Word that will create a more exciting, intimate relationship with your spouse.

Growth Exercises

1. Tonight after the kids are in bed or when you and your mate can be alone, sit down together and discuss what you have read in this chapter. Maybe you haven't really talked for a long time. Begin tonight. Analyze and discuss yourselves as unique individuals and list areas in which you complement each other (husband is weak in one area where wife is strong, and so forth). You've probably noticed this already, but it is helpful to write it down. Can you accept each other as unique individuals? When was the last time you said thank you to the Lord for your husband or wife? Do it tonight.

2. The following exercise will help to focus on some of the important principles you examined in chapter one. Review what you have read in this chapter by discussing these main points with your mate.
   Adam and Eve were:
   Created in God's image.
   Created to exercise dominion over the living things of the earth.
   Created to help or serve each other.
   Victims of a satanic wedge.
   Blessed through God's desire to commit husbands and wives to a biblical sense of teamwork.

> Restored to fellowship with God through Christ and the Holy Spirit. Granted a freedom in Christ to provide equal opportunity in the marriage for the expression of each partner's individual personhood.

3. Write a brief paragraph describing what these principles mean to you as you seek to be a godly husband or wife.

Additional Reading

Linda Dillow. *Creative Counterpart.* Nashville: Thomas Nelson, Inc., 1978.

John Mac Arthur, Jr. *The Family.* Chicago: Moody Press, 1982.

Charles R. Swindoll. *Strike the Original Match.* Portland, Ore.: Multnomah Press, 1980.

2

Intimacy: *A Goal for Marriage*

One word can summarize the content of the following poem:

I am so happy with you
I can discuss all my thoughts, or
I don't have to say anything;
You always understand.

I am so relaxed with you
I don't need to pretend.
I don't need to look good;
You accept me for what I am.

I am so strong with you
I depend on you for love.
But I live my own life;
You give me confidence to succeed.

The word is *intimacy.*

Intimacy is the ultimate goal for your marriage. Each chapter in this book aims to help you achieve this goal. However, much misunderstanding exists concerning what intimacy really is, and we first will look at some of the misconceptions.

Erroneous Concepts of Intimacy

Intimacy is sometimes understood to be the dynamic interlocking of every area of a couple's life. Definitions such as this can be misunderstood. Some people may suppose that intimacy in marriage involves surrendering their own personalities and uniqueness. This is wrong. God has made each person unique. No one ever will be exactly like you. David understood this and exclaimed: "I will praise thee: for I am fearfully and wonderfully made: marvelous are thy works; and that my soul knoweth right well" (Ps. 139:14).

God has made your mate unique; no one will ever be exactly like him or her again. Marriage involves two unique individuals who voluntarily enter into covenant with each other. To complement each other, both must firmly recognize their unique value as persons. In addition to the natural endowments each believer already possesses, at the new birth each receives a special gift with which to serve God and others (see 1 Cor. 12:4–11 and Rom. 12:6–8 for lists of those gifts).

Husbands and wives should freely commit their personal resources to the development of the marriage team. Their ability to meet the demands of life is greatly enhanced when both unique sets of abilities are allowed to blossom and find full positions of strength in the marriage. The proper balance of togetherness and space allows them to function efficiently for the glory of God and the ultimate good of each contributing member.

Submission is a hot subject in Christian circles. According to Ephesians 5:22, the wife must submit to her husband. Some men take license with this passage and use it to support a view of leadership that turns the wife into a glorified doormat. They imply that her opinions and needs do not count. She has no rights but should take care of the kids, the house, and other "wifely duties."

This view of submission is tragic. The team is impoverished when one of its major resources is reduced to impotency. The idea that the female is not a contributor but merely a passive vessel waiting to be filled places an unbelievable burden on the male. He robs himself of a major source of strength if he reduces the female with her talents to a noncontributor.

Men who verbalize this erroneous view seldom mention Ephesians 5:18, 21: "Be filled with the Spirit . . . submitting yourselves one to another in the fear of God. Wives, submit yourselves unto your own husbands, as unto the Lord."

Submit to implies an attitude of respect that is mandated for all believers, not just wives. Submission is not a doctrine for females only; it is universal, for men and women. Submission is not unilateral; it is not required in all situations. Submission can never be used as an excuse to violate a clear principle of Scripture. Commitment to God and his Word takes precedence over any other chain of command (Acts 5:29).

Spiritual men value their wives (1 Peter 3:7) and recognize in them one of God's greatest gifts. As they get to know their wives, they come to appreciate the unique ways in which God has gifted them. Such husbands respect those gifts and look for opportunities to help strengthen them. Wise men know that building their wives results in the strengthening of the team. Ultimately, the male who strengthens his wife strengthens himself (Eph. 5:28, 29).

This is the 1990s. Radical feminists emphasize the rights of women. They frequently look down on the institution of marriage and view it as oppressive for women. They maintain, rather, that each individual in the marriage should be disengaged from the other; she should keep her name and her checkbook. The emphasis is on separateness over conscious commitment to oneness.

The emphasis on individual strengths can be detrimental when it results in each one doing his or her own thing. I have defined intimacy as oneness with healthy separateness. Healthy separateness means that one personality does not dominate the other, but neither does it push individuality to the point of disengagement. C. S. Lewis captured the balance between separateness and oneness when he wrote: "The most precious gift that marriage gave me was the constant impact of something very close and intimate yet all the time unmistakably other, resistant—in a word, real."

Males and females who forsake the biblical concept of the marriage team will rob themselves of one of this world's greatest joys. Men who desire wives who are doormats create their own misery.

They live with a shallow imitation of the divine intention for marriage. Females who cut themselves off from their husbands miss a source of great enrichment. A world composed of men and women who miss the balance of separateness and oneness is a world filled with sexual confusion and an overabundance of poor communication between males and females.

Intimacy and *sex* are two terms that are frequently used interchangeably. How unfortunate! Sex, no matter how great, is not intimacy. Sex is often a physical act devoid of intimacy.

Intimacy is the foundation for a healthy sexual relationship. When two individuals with healthy identities voluntarily share the sexual experience within the context of covenantal commitment, sex is an experience of dignity, sanctity, and joy.

Intimacy: *Three Areas*

Paul closes his first letter to the Thessalonians with a prayer for the sanctification of their total personalities. In his prayer he identifies the human personality's constituent parts when he says: "And the very God of peace sanctify you wholly; and I pray God your whole spirit and soul and body be preserved blameless unto the coming of our Lord Jesus Christ" (1 Thess. 5:23).

This prayer suggests three areas of personality in which to develop intimacy: spirit, soul, and body.

Spiritual Intimacy

It is important to consider the price for ignoring any of these areas. A couple may have a good physical relationship but ignore the development of the spiritual area. This empty dimension in the relationship provides a space for temptation where Satan can work to destroy the relationship. The person lacking spiritual interaction, even though receiving physical love, may be attracted to a person who fulfills the spiritual need, an attraction that may ultimately result in an extramarital relationship. This can be prevented if both married partners recognize the need for a relationship that covers all the areas that are important in a fully developed personality.

Couples should be drawn together as they grow in their spiritual relationship with the Lord. Studying Scripture together provides them with the opportunity to check their attitudes and actions against the authority of biblical principles. Praying together insures keeping short accounts with each other and with God. Partners cannot pray effectively when they are at odds with their mates (1 Peter 3:7). Unresolved areas of conflict hinder true prayer and should not be tolerated by partners who desire to see their relationships growing.

Spiritual exercises need not be complex. Often husbands feel they must provide their wives with a full thirty-minute message. This is not necessary and often not desirable. Prayers between couples should be simple and from the heart. The simple reading of Scripture and the sharing of ideas on what it means will suffice.

Church attendance and fellowship with other Christians is very important. However, the primary source of spiritual enrichment should be derived from the interaction of the couple. They should gladly accept the responsibility for enriching one another in the spiritual area. (Such a responsibility only heightens the tragedy of the Christian married to a non-Christian.)

Intimacy of Soul or Intellect

An intimacy of soul is also of great importance. The couple must learn to share ideas, thoughts, emotions, and volitional force as it shapes their decisions and directions.

Intellectual intimacy is derived from consciously sharing ideas. The thoughts that serve to shape and direct the spouses' lives are openly discussed. Neither one is possessed of a secret agenda that obscures or confuses directions that are in the best interest of the team.

Intellectual intimacy is a great challenge. I have frequently found that I am not careful to share my thoughts with Peg. I will share the beginning of the thought process and the end with her, then find she has missed all the in-between thoughts. I am impatient with her when she doesn't understand my conclusions. How could she? She has not had the opportunity to ponder the information that I have. I have learned that this style of communicating can really hurt intimacy.

The achievement of soul intimacy also requires the sharing of intimate feelings. Men often have been taught not to express their emotions. The "macho" man is emotionally cool and always controls his feelings. This cultural stereotype does great harm to American males and has deeply diminished their ability to build intimate relationships.

Couples enjoy an increasing quality of intimacy when they learn to be emotionally present with each other, when each partner feels comfortable expressing personal needs. They must feel safe in the other's presence and then take the risk of exposing their vulnerability. Intimacy is not possible without vulnerability. I look at my wife as an island of safety in a world of storms. I can share my thoughts and feelings openly with her, knowing that she always receives them with sensitivity and love. She will not always agree with my interpretation of events. However, just knowing that she is there to listen and love is a source of great stability for me.

Mates choose with their wills to love one another unconditionally and permanently through attitude, word, and action. Volition or will is an important part of intimacy. The will to relate is a necessary precondition for the development of intimacy. Intimacy grows in a climate of trust based on commitment to fidelity and continuity (Song of Sol. 8:6, Prov. 31:11). Aaron Beck has recently written a book titled *Love Is Never Enough*. He strongly argues the point that even non-Christian couples require a commitment to fidelity if they hope to achieve a satisfying relationship.

Physical Intimacy

Physical intimacy does not stand independent of an intimacy of spirit and soul. It is deeply affected by the quality of intimacy a couple experiences in these areas. Sexual intimacy within marriage is meant to be a celebration (Song of Sol. 2). Participation in the sex act completes, consoles, and unites husbands and wives.

The development of intimacy requires the wholehearted cooperation of both partners. Nature abhors a vacuum. Dig a hole in the ground, and water will rush in to fill it. Leave an empty spot in a relationship, and something will fill it. Often Satan can use that empty place to begin to attack the marriage. To the best of their ability couples must make certain that they have left no vacuums in their relationships.

Barriers to Intimacy

Intimacy can grow and flourish only in a place of safety. The close of this chapter considers some barriers to intimacy that make individuals and couples feel unsafe. They shut down their willingness to be vulnerable.

A lack of trust is a real barrier to intimacy. Trust creates mutual reliance, and when it is absent reliance is impossible. Seeds of mistrust grow to destroy a relationship.

A lack of a realistic and balanced self-image will be a barrier to intimacy. Self-image is basic to developing relationships with others. If I can value myself, as God's unique creation, I will be in a better position to accept and value others. An honest self-image begins with Romans 12:3: "For I say, through the grace given unto me, to every man that is among you, not to think of himself more highly than he ought to think; but to think soberly, according as God hath dealt to every man the measure of faith."

Many people suffer from low self-worth and have extra need of other people's approval; their sense of self-worth is built on the strokes they receive from others. But Paul believes Christians' greatest value is found in the fact that God has freely chosen to be involved in our lives. God has given us a measure of faith, and therein lies our unique value. He is ours and we are his. He loves us. Our basic sense of security and value as persons is really derived from our relationship with him. This keeps us from having either overinflated or underinflated views of ourselves and our personal worth.

Mishandled hostility greatly damages intimacy. Anger almost always grows from lifelong habits learned from childhood experiences and parental examples. Over a period of time, such explosions result in emotional distancing. An extremely hostile person needs, through extensive formal counseling, training in anger management. The victim of such anger must be careful to avoid developing a "root of bitterness" (Heb. 12:15).

Strangely, the perpetrators of explosive angry behavior seem quickly to forget it happened. They frequently "go right on as if it never happened," some verbally abused spouses maintain. Rather then risk a repeat performance, the abused spouse may also ostensibly "forget it." Nothing ever gets resolved in this forgetting atmosphere. Mistrust grows, and intimacy at any level becomes less and less possible.

"Godly" husbands also may misdirect their anger over personal hurts and frustrations and take out their bad feelings on their wives. This common phenomenon must be faced, recognized, and dealt with in a calm moment and not by a shouting match. Frequently partners enflame their angry mates and escalate the cycle of violence by arguing with them during angry episodes. Intimacy is possible only when two people learn how to say the word *sorry* and apply healthy doses of forgiveness to wounds inflicted during careless moments of speech.

Intimacy is the goal in marriage. God intended for couples to experience intimacy in every area of life: the emotional, spiritual, and physical. The next chapters will discuss the foundation for intimacy (commitment) and the seven pillars of commitment through which intimacy is achieved.

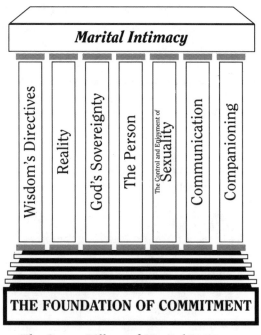

The Seven Pillars of Marital Intimacy

Growth Exercises

1. Tonight you and your partner should sit down and attempt to strengthen
   your relationship. Take a risk and together begin to explore areas where
   you think there might be barriers to becoming more intimate. When you
   find a barrier of mutual concern, focus on it and discuss practical ways of
   breaking down the barrier so you can be more intimate. As you take
   practical steps, trust the Lord to give you victory, as a couple, to overcome each barrier. He is faithful.

   To help you get started you might want to discuss the following statements describing intimacy. Intimacy is:

   Oneness with healthy separateness.
   The sharing of our minds, emotions, wills, bodies, and spirits based on
        a balance of oneness and separateness that is only possible when
        we have a clear sense of who we are as individuals.

2. Following your initial discussion, reinforce your resolve by reading and
   reviewing, whenever necessary, the following valuable ingredients of intimacy.
   a. Mutual Respect
      1 Peter 3:7: "Likewise, ye husbands, dwell with them according to
         knowledge, giving honor unto the wife, as unto the weaker ves-
         sel, and as being heirs together of the grace of life; that your
         prayers be not hindered."
      Do you increasingly find in your relationship the following indicators of
         mutual respect?

      You value the other's opinions, criticisms, and advice.
      You treat each other as equals—or better (Phil. 2:3).
      You communicate with, not at, each other.
      You are trustful and confident of each other.
      You admire each other's strengths and respect each other's dif-
           ferences.

   b. Interdependence
      Amos 3:3: "Can two walk together except they be agreed?"

Ephesians 5:21: "Submitting yourselves one to another in the fear of God."

Do you increasingly find in your relationship the following indicators of interdependence?

There is a need for agreement, yet room for differences.

You have the ability to concede and the freedom to choose.

There is a need for dependence on your mate, yet not the need to control him or her.

You cherish both your time together and your time apart.

You would not ask the other to do that which you would not do yourself.

A mutual submission, not a topdog/underdog dynamic, dominates your relationship.

c. Defenselessness

1 Peter 3:8–9: "Finally, be ye all of one mind, having compassion one of another, love as brethren, be pitiful, be courteous: not rendering evil for evil."

Do you increasingly find in your relationship the following indicators of a nondefensive spirit?

You can expose your feelings at the risk of rejection.

You are willing to risk hurt for the goal of achieving the reward of intimacy and growth.

You are strengthening your attitude of trust.

You encourage rather than argue with your mate.

You are willing to leave yourself vulnerable.

You try to see your mate's point of view.

You believe that the meek really are blessed.

d. Guileless Motivation

2 Corinthians 4:2: "But [we] have renounced the hidden things of dishonesty, not walking in craftiness, nor handling the word of God deceitfully; but by manifestation of the truth commending ourselves to every man's conscience in the sight of God."

Do you increasingly find in your relationship the following indicators of a guileless spirit?

Honesty is a priority with you.

You value transparency and genuineness.

You actively avoid manipulating others for personal goals.

You safeguard against portraying yourself in the most favorable light.

You value the truth, even if it hurts; but you do not use it as a weapon to hurt the other one.

You believe God is witnessing every transaction between you and your mate, and you always try to please him or her (while not allowing that to diminish yourself).

e. Personal Identity

1 John 3:2: "Beloved, now are we the sons of God, and it doth not yet appear what we shall be: but we know that, when he shall appear, we shall be like him; for we shall see him as he is."

Your real identity is only discovered when you have a personal relationship with your heavenly Father through Jesus Christ.

Your sense of personal identity is accurate only if it is formed within the context of an awareness of who God truly is and who you are in comparison to him (2 Cor. 3:18).

Your sense of personal identity can be either enhanced or muddied by your mate.

Your ultimate identity is derived from the knowledge that God has wonderfully made you (Ps. 139:13–16).

3. Read Ecclesiastes 4:8–12, which tells you that you are created to be intimate. To be intimate you must first be loved and accepted. Even if other people do not love you, you can know the love and acceptance of God. The knowledge of that love and the personal experience of that love is the only sufficient foundation upon which an intimate relationship can be founded. As you have your Bible study together during the coming months, add to those listed here other texts and passages that reinforce the principles in this chapter.

Additional Reading

Lucy and Dennis Guernsey. *Real Life Marriage.* Waco: Word, 1987.

C. S. Lewis. *The Four Loves.* New York: Harcourt Brace Jovanovich, 1960.

Norman Wright. *Marital Counseling.* New York: Harper and Row, 1981.

3

Commitment:
The Foundation for Marriage

Abraham Maslow is a psychologist who teaches that self-actu-alization is the highest goal people can pursue. Although he is somewhat vague about the exact content of self-actualization, it is clear that the heart of his proposed goal is self. A generation of college students have studied Maslow, adopted his goal, and trav-eled up what has been called the "Maslovian escalator."

Self-fulfillment is as old as Satan (Isa. 14, Ezek. 28), Adam and Eve. Each successive generation has shared in the enthusiasm for the pursuit of those things that satisfy selfish desires. The dif-ference in the 1980s was the legitimizing of that selfish pursuit. Society at large now accepts the fact that everyone is out for number one, which is viewed in some sense as the American way.

The consequences of these attitudes for marriage relationships have been catastrophic. Many people now enter marriage with previous commitments that make shams of their wedding promises. They have committed all their energies to self-fulfill-ment, and marriage is only one more way of filling their selfish desires.

It is beyond the ability of such persons to fulfill the request made in Song of Solomon 8:6: "Set me as a seal upon thine heart, as a seal upon thine arm: for love is strong as death; jealousy is cruel as the grave: the coals thereof are coals of fire, which hath a most vehement flame."

The Nature of Christian Marriage

Marriage is, among other things, a social contract. In the marriage of Isaac and Rebekah we see an example of its social dimension. The marriage was arranged by Abraham's servant and Rebekah's family (Gen. 24). Rebekah's family gave consent, and Abraham's servant carefully followed the directions of his master. The marriage was consummated out of consideration for these social structures.

In my ministry with college students, the subject of foregoing marriage and simply living together inevitably comes up. I have consistently pointed out that this is an unbiblical notion. It ignores the fact that Christian believers, as well as unbelievers, live within a social context and have responsibilities to that society (Rom. 13:1–7).

Marriage involves a contractual act by which two individuals enter into a binding agreement. The contract is a function of the social culture in which the couple lives. It receives its particular form from that culture. Obeying the form is a dimension of rendering unto "Caesar" (the state) the things that belong to him. This obedience also brings the protection and benefits of the state to that relationship. Laws in each state clearly define requirements for the legal processes, such as blood tests, obtaining the marriage license, and other details. Obeying "Caesar" and fulfilling the demands of a social contract is a way of showing love for a spouse.

Marriage also involves a spiritual covenant. The spiritual nature of marriage is discussed by Paul in Ephesians 5:22–24:

Wives submit yourselves unto your own husbands, as unto the Lord. For the husband is the head of the wife, even as Christ is the head of the church: and he is the saviour of the body. Therefore as the church is subject unto Christ, so let the wives be to their own husbands in every thing."

The covenant that Christ made with his church is permanent. It is unalterable and may not be abolished. Marriage is to be viewed in the same light. In Malachi 2:11–16 the prophet summarizes God's attitude toward those who treat lightly the marriage covenant. Malachi says that God views violation of the marriage covenant as treachery. Treachery against the wife of a man's youth is particularly abhorred by God. Men ought always to guard against the desire to participate in such treachery.

Marriage, then, is a commitment that involves Jesus Christ, the husband, and the wife. It may be that Solomon had this divine arrangement in mind when he said a threefold cord is not quickly broken (Eccles. 4:12).

Two things are clearly possible as a result of a committed marital relationship. First, the couple may experience reward. Solomon said: "Two are better than one; for they have a good reward for their labor" (Eccles. 4:9). The reward gained through solid commitment is the joy of sharing the agony and ecstasy of the journey with a committed other. Second, the world is presented with an illustration of God's loving commitment to reaching and keeping his creatures. In marital commitment we see modeled the unalterable love of God. God depends on Christians to show the world his deep love for those he has created.

Commitment: *What Does it Mean?*

The word *commitment* is not used in the Bible, but its derivatives *committed* and *commit* are. The words have two meanings in the Greek: "doing or practicing something," and "delivering or entrusting something to a person." Commitment involves the binding or pledging of oneself to a particular course of action.

Commitment implies a choice based on reasoning. The act of entrusting oneself to another should be supported by sound reasoning. Men or women should be able to offer to themselves and others sound, rational arguments for why this is a healthy relationship and should be expected to flourish. Commitment also involves volitional consent; persons will themselves into relationships. When the will to relate to another person is supported by reasons that validate the goodness or the fit, then we may reasonably expect to see a stable long-term relationship.

Commitment implies a pledge by each spouse to fidelity for life. When commitment is present, a couple enters into an irrevocable covenant. They pledge their faithfulness, regardless of circumstances. It has something of the spirit of Hernando Cortez when in 1519 he landed his troops at Vera Cruz, Mexico. The more than six thousand men were irrevocably committed to their task of conquering the new land for the mother country. When Cortez set fire to the vessels that had brought them, there was no retreat. That kind of "no retreat" commitment in marriage is indicated when Jesus said in Matthew 19:5: "For this cause shall a man leave father and mother and shall cleave to his wife."

Commitment is the unconditional acceptance of the other partner. It is the absence of rejection and means each will always be there, no matter what. Commitment is the surrender of personal pleasure and comfort. It demands that each desires to pursue the best for the other and guard all actions in the light of that commitment. Commitment is best understood as it is modeled in the life of Jesus Christ.

Commitment costs something; dependability has a price tag. Consistently encouraging a partner, giving the gift of sympathetic understanding, and saying no to personal desires cuts against the grain of the selfish nature. Commitment means organizing one's time, thoughts, and resources for the benefit of others. It means the surrender of a measure of personal freedom and rights.

The bondservant is discussed in the Book of Exodus. He is a model of commitment when he says: "I love my master, my wife, and my children; I will not go out free" (Exod. 21:5). Every seventh year all Hebrew servants were set free. The bondservant, motivated by love, freely chose to remain within the context of his commitments. Paul suggests in Romans 1:1 that the bondservant, with his selfless commitment to others, models the quality of commitment believers should have to Jesus Christ.

The committed couple will try to spend time together on a daily basis and share their thoughts. Marriage is best viewed as the union of two friends.

Friends handle differences with a minimum of anger and manage all their dealings with care and fondness. Constructive interaction is always the goal. Energy that threatens the friendship will be captured and banished to the seas of self-control.

Commitment requires self-control and a willingness to compromise. Partners must always try to surrender their desire for self-fulfillment and attempt to promote the best interests of the other. They must seek concretely to meet real needs in their partners' lives (1 Peter 3:1–7).

Coleman captures the desire to focus on the good of the partner in the following poem:

> Turn the radio off. Put the paper down.
> Give the TV a rest.
> I want to hear you—and hear you alone.
> Send the children out to play. Take the
> telephone off the hook.
> I want to listen to your voice—and yours
> alone.
>
> I want to hear how you feel and know what you think.
> Tell me what your heart feels, what your mind
> wonders and how your soul hungers.
> Put the car keys back. Close the door. Be
> later for your next appointment.
> Share with me what makes you laugh. Remind
> me what makes you upset.
> I want to hear your voice and keep in touch
> with your spirit.

> William Coleman
> *Knit Together*
> © Bethany House, 1987.
> Used with permission.

Roadblocks to Commitment

As a newly married couple we discovered many roadblocks to commitment. My own selfishness and egoism were the primary enemies of my ability to model commitment in my marriage. I knew the concept and I felt the need to model its content.

Frequently, however, I would retreat into silence and muse over how impossible she was. I was immature and selfish.

Selfish persons do not consider their mates' needs. They are committed to themselves. They are dominated by a previous commitment to their personal satisfaction and they seek to use others as resources to meet their personal needs. In bondage to their sin natures, particularly their ego needs, they are powerless to model the attributes of the bondservant.

Selfish persons are often dominated by patterns that were formed in childhood. They never have enough; they constantly demand more. They often justify their behaviors by saying that the present state of the world demands such actions.

Jesus, Lord of heaven and earth, Creator and owner of all things, "took upon him the form of a servant" (Phil. 2:5–8). He—God—was willing to suffer humiliation at the hands of his creatures, motivated by love. Christians must choose to adopt the identical mindset. It is a matter of will. They have a choice about what kinds of persons they will be, with no acceptable excuses derived from supposedly faulty parentage.

The only lasting cure for egoistic selfishness that I know of is regeneration. The tragic egomaniac is without resources to unshackle himself from his narcissistic covenant with self apart from regeneration. Only through obedience to the Holy Spirit, received in regeneration, will such a person find power to break the maniacal grip of selfishness. The fact that the pattern may have been learned in the family of origin only serves to heighten the need for the Spirit's power. Through becoming part of a new family (the family of God), experiencing God's agape love, and mobilizing the Spirit's power this person can be transformed.

The tragic consequences of selfishness are summed up well in the following poem:

> We've read a dozen books about marriage.
> Even taken a test or two just to see how we
> were doing. Went to a seminar, listened to a
> tape, made notes so we could discuss it later.
> We wanted to learn how to hold together, how
> to make it work, how to be close.

We are a progressive couple, aware partners,
sensitive companions.

Through it all we found a basic—an ingredient
that held everything else together.
Lovers who are thoughtful have a beautiful
relationship. Partners who are selfish tear a
marriage to shreds.
Thoughtfulness carries its own splendor.
Selfishness is as ugly as an oyster.
No matter what other strengths we have going,
none will cover the stench of selfishness.
Thoughtfulness carries a beauty that begins
inside and pushes to the surface.

> William Coleman
> *Knit Together*
> © Bethany House, 1987.
> Used with permission.

An unforgiving spirit is a powerful roadblock to commitment. Forgiveness is essential if people are to go on as marriage partners. Holding grudges destroys intimacy. Paul says in Ephesians 4:32: "Be ye kind one to another, tenderhearted, forgiving one another, even as God for Christ's sake hath forgiven you."

We were headed for Florida on a winter vacation trip. It was Sunday morning, and we decided to find a church. We stopped at a little church in Georgia. The preacher did a fine job. He spoke of a woman who came with her husband for marriage counseling. The counseling had no sooner begun when she broke into a hysterical recitation of all her husband's past wrongs. The husband complained that she was burying him with her "historicalness." The preacher thought he meant "hystericalness" and proceeded to correct the husband. However, the husband meant "historicalness" and proceeded to tell the preacher that every time they tried to discuss issues, she would bring up every mistake he had made from day one of their marriage. "Historicalness" can ruin a marriage. Marriage partners must learn to hang a "no fishing" sign over past failures and extend forgiveness to their mates.

Frequently Christians confuse forgiving and forgetting. I believe only God can forgive and forget. The human mind is like a giant computer. It never really forgets anything. Sometimes well-meaning believers try to forgive but reason that since they still remember a grievous wrong they have not forgiven it.

I have forgiven another when I do not allow what he has done to determine my decisions about my responses to him. I choose to give no power to my memories of past wrongs. I remember them occasionally; however, by faith, I reckon them to be past and I do not let them play a role in the present relationship. Then, and only then, am I obeying Ephesians 4:26 by not letting the sun go down on my wrath.

Unfaithfulness is another powerful roadblock to commitment. Unfaithfulness is the habitual violation of covenant that destroys the trust on which any happy relationship must be founded. The virtuous woman of Proverbs 31 is of such great value because the heart of her husband "doth safely trust in her" (Prov. 31:11). No marriage can or should last when unfaithfulness is continuously present.

A lack of effort to invest quality time in a relationship is another serious roadblock to the maintenance of commitment. Couples need to regulate their time. We live in a microwave society where meals are possible in a matter of minutes. With less time involved in routine duties of the home, careful budgeting of time will make allowances for time together. In the family that includes one or more children, such time does not happen accidentally. Joy Rice Martin, in years of fewer "instant mixes," used to take a snack out to the workshop room where her husband was at work, and after they shared the food she quietly sat watching him. She also related before a ladies' retreat crowd their secret of special times together in days when they "lived on a shoestring." They went to a restaurant and ordered two cups of coffee, one piece of pie, and two forks. Taking the time and equally dividing one piece of pie under such circumstances is a powerful metaphor for a quality commitment that will create an enduring marriage.

Committed and Going! Where?

Commitment needs to be joined to goals. In the remaining chapters of this book we will be looking at the directions couples should go in their commitment. Following are a few preliminary suggestions about the directions that should flow from commitment.

First, couples need to commit themselves mutually to the fulfillment of one another's needs. People are not always as complex as they seem. They tend to feel positive about a situation where their needs are being met and negative about a situation where they are not. I frequently ask couples to make a list of the needs in their lives that their partners are meeting. When I get a blank sheet of paper back I know the marriage is in trouble.

Second, they need to commit themselves to the promotion of growth in their relationship. To accomplish this commitment it is best to focus on the personal growth of the partner. Peter admonished husbands to dwell with their wives "according to knowledge" (1 Peter 3:7).

Husbands should make the growth of their wives a primary focus for the investment of their time and energy. That investment will pay rich dividends. I frequently see young men come to seminary and forget this focus. They expand their minds, expend their energies, and forget to focus on their wives. This is a mistake that all too frequently bears tragic fruit.

Husbands and wives should delight in seeing one another grow. They should restrain their impulses, direct their schedules, and invest their energies for the express purpose of facilitating the growth of their mates. Growing persons appreciate the agape love from their partners who make their growth a high level item on the marital agenda. The truly committed partner is happiest when the other partner is finding great pleasure, comfort, and satisfaction in the relationship.

Third, a need exists to clarify role expectations within the marriage. Few things do greater damage to a marriage than one partner's failure to do what the other expected. Frequently I hear young couples say, "He is not at all what I thought he was" or "I expected you would do this."

Often during courtship nonverbalized expectations evolve. She expects that he will be responsible and keep his side of the bedroom clean. She never verbalizes that expectation. She assumes that her expectations will be realized. She assumes that he will be as good a carpenter as her father. He assumes she will cook like his mother and pick up after him just as his mother did.

Imagine the hurt and anger when she realizes that he isn't picking up his clothes. He isn't repairing things around the house. She isn't cooking like Mom. She isn't putting up with his irresponsibility.

Each time one of these he–isn't—she–isn't thoughts lodges in the brain, anger and resentment are reinforced in the relationship.

Role expectations need to be resolved early in the relationship. Listening, understanding, acceptance, and compromise, as well as change, will be necessary for the strengthening of commitment. A commitment to develop complementary and fulfilling role behavior is vital if two persons are to go on to intimacy.

Conclusion

Perhaps your commitment to your marriage has waned lately. The busyness of life has crept in, and now the two of you are merely existing together; each is doing his or her own thing. Maybe roadblocks have sprung up. Deal with these roadblocks right away. You have the power, through Christ, to eliminate them completely. You can replace them with a deep commitment to your partner and to fulfilling his or her needs. Commitment has a big price tag attached to it, but it's worth every cent. The goal? Intimacy. That's the payoff. You may have to identify and repent of individual sin to get back on track.

This week—tonight—you can choose, as a couple, to renew your commitment to each other. And you can do it in a tangible way. Perhaps you will choose to sit down and say those words of commitment to your spouse, express your love and assurance of loyalty and confidence in him or her. Or maybe you'll send your spouse a note to that effect with a rose attached. Maybe you should read aloud your original vows to each other. You can undoubtedly think of something creative to do to renew your commitment. There can be no growth in your relationship as long as there is doubt about your commitment to your marriage.

Growth Exercises

The Bible contains several principles regarding commitment in a marriage. Working through the following questions will serve to enhance your understanding of the importance of commitment for your marriage, relationships, and personal growth.

1. Read together Song of Solomon 8:6, 7. Discuss your answers to these questions:

   What, do you think, Solomon wants couples to learn from this passage?

   Why, do you think, should the seal be on both heart and arm?

   How is the beginning of jealousy related to the absence or presence of the seal?

   What is Solomon teaching about the nature of love in the passage?

2. The meaning of commitment is modeled for us by Jesus Christ (see 1 Peter 2:23). Read that passage together.

3. People mature when someone loves them enough to remain committed to them through their failures. Read together Acts 15:36–41; 2 Timothy 4:11.

   In a sentence or two describe what commitment from Barnabas meant in the life of Mark. Do you tend to be a Barnabas or a Paul for your husband or wife?

4. Read Ephesians 1:13. Can you think of any similarity between the use of the seal here and its use in Song of Solomon 8:6? Does that commitment imply an irreversible dimension in a relationship?

5. Read Luke 9:62. What one word would you use to summarize what the passage teaches you about commitment?

6. Read John 3:16. Commitment requires giving; it costs something. What are you giving to your marriage to demonstrate your commitment?

7. Read Exodus 21:1–6. Commitment is painful at times. Is your commitment to your marriage causing you discomfort, distress, or real pain? Each spouse should list one or two ideas for working together to minimize or avoid the unpleasant aspects of commitment.

8. What might you expect if you are really committed to someone? What might you expect from someone who is really committed to you?

4

Commitment to Wisdom's Directives

What do you think about when you hear the term *wisdom?* Some people think of Aristotle, Plato, and Socrates. Few people think of the Bible; yet the greatest treasury of wisdom available to humanity is found in the Bible. The Bible places great emphasis on acquiring wisdom. Look at the following texts:

Proverbs 24:3–4: "Through wisdom is an house builded; and by understanding it is established; and by knowledge shall the chambers be filled with all precious and pleasant riches."

Proverbs 4:5: "Get wisdom, get understanding: forget it not; neither decline from the words of my mouth."

Psalm 111:10: "The fear of the LORD is the beginning of wisdom; a good understanding have all they that do his commandments: his praise endureth forever."

James 1:5: "If any of you lack wisdom, let him ask of God, that giveth to all men liberally and upbraideth not; and it shall be given him."

What is wisdom? Wisdom is not numbered among the natural possessions of humans. It is something persons get from God. Wisdom is the ability to conceive creative solutions, rooted in biblical truth, for life's problems. Wisdom is a prerequisite for building an intimate marriage. Wisdom's directives, unveiled in

God's Word and faithfully practiced ensure success for couples who desire to achieve intimacy.

Christian couples must daily apply the counsel of wisdom to the details of life and let it shape their attitudes and behavior in every situation. Wisdom is the use of knowledge in a practical and successful way. The first prerequisite for wisdom is a right relationship with God.

There are several sources of godly wisdom. Wisdom is incarnated in Jesus Christ, wisdom is in the Scriptures, and wisdom is bestowed as a special gift from God.

Without a commitment to God and the wisdom that he alone gives, couples may not hope to build strong marriages. This life is filled with danger. Only God's wisdom can direct them away from foolishness and into the path that leads to success as God defines it.

Wisdom Is in the Son

Wisdom is incarnated in Jesus Christ. Paul states in 1 Corinthians 1:29–31: "No flesh should glory in his presence. But of him are ye in Christ Jesus, who of God is made unto us wisdom, and righteousness, and sanctification, and redemption: that according as it is written, He that glorieth, let him glory in the Lord."

Christians are dependent. They dare not imagine they have the wisdom necessary to solve all of life's complex problems. At times they are burdened by their sense of inadequacy. However, the sense of inadequacy is replaced by a sense of joy as they realize that God has redeemed them.

Redemption means more than salvation from hell. In redemption, the Son of God, who is the wisdom of God, dwells in his people.

Christians are indwelt by wisdom. They glory in the Lord, knowing that in Christ they have been provided with wisdom to make right decisions and pursue right goals. They have a responsibility to this indwelling wisdom.

God's children must develop a relationship with Jesus. The result of a strong relationship with him is a growing conviction that they can trust God continuously. Paul reminded Timothy of this rich blessing when he said in 2 Timothy 1:12: "For the which cause I also suffer these things: nevertheless I am not ashamed: for I know whom I have believed, and am persuaded that he is able to keep that which I have committed unto him against that day."

Husbands and wives must individually accept the responsibility for their personal relationship with Jesus Christ. Paul's faith could serve as an inspiration for Timothy, but it could not become Timothy's faith unless Timothy made it his own. Sometimes marital intimacy will suffer because one of the partners refuses to accept responsibility for walking in obedience to wisdom's directives. The obedient partner must continue to be a faithful model of commitment to Christ in spite of the lack of obedience in the mate. Sometimes that will soften a disobedient partner, but sometimes it will serve to harden him or her. The obedient partner's walk is guided by the certain direction of wisdom found in God's Word. This walk is not abandoned because of a negative response from another person.

Wisdom Is in Scripture

Timothy had his problems and seemed overwhelmed at times by fear and anxiety. Paul deeply loved this young man and spoke prescriptively to him in his second letter to Timothy: "For God hath not given us the spirit of fear, but of power, and of love, and of a sound mind" (2 Tim. 1:7).

Paul's approach to helping Timothy serves to remind us all how important the Bible is to our growth as Christians. Paul said in 2 Timothy 3:15–17: "From a child thou hast known the holy scriptures, which are able to make thee wise unto salvation through faith which is in Christ Jesus."

"All scripture is given by inspiration of God, and is profitable for doctrine, for reproof, for correction, for instruction, for righteousness: that the man of God may be perfect, thoroughly furnished unto all good works."

Reading and applying the Bible to our lives is wise. I remember when I first became a believer. I walked the fields of a small New York farm reading the Bible. I couldn't get enough of the Scriptures. The more I read them the more I became settled in my faith. Bible study must be a vital reality in the life of the believer. Peter said: "As newborn babes, desire the sincere milk of the word, that ye may grow thereby" (1 Peter 2:2). A consistent relationship with the Word of God is one of the marks of a true believer.

Several books in the Bible are known as books of wisdom. Proverbs, Ecclesiastes, and Song of Solomon are three of these wisdom books. In Ecclesiastes we find a wise method for studying God's Word. Solomon gives these directions in Ecclesiastes 12:9–11: "Because the preacher was wise, he still taught the people knowledge; yea, he gave good heed, and sought out, and set in order many proverbs. The preacher sought to find out acceptable words: and that which was written was upright, even words of truth. The words of the wise are as goads, and as nails fastened by the masters of assemblies, which are given from one shepherd."

The preacher here is not a pulpiteer in today's sense. The term denotes a convener of an assembly. It could be a mother assembling her children for family worship or a teacher assembling his class. This text is addressed to whoever brings a group of people together for the purpose of instruction.

This teacher should rely on wisdom from above. She should thank God for inspiration, but she should be willing to labor and to perspire over the Word of God. Bible study is hard work. Preachers who wait to be inspired and avoid the hard work of preparation are not commended in this text.

The wise teacher recognizes all of the Bible as truth from God, the Shepherd of Israel. The truth both secures and makes uncomfortable. Wise teachers prick and prod with goads and secure and stabilize with nails. They sweat over the Word of God. They set the content of God's Word in categorical order and suit their texts to the meeting of legitimate human needs.

Wisdom Is Bestowed as a Gift from God

This statement may seem blasphemous, but sometimes having the Son and the Scriptures is not enough. Christians need a special endowment of divine wisdom. God has made provision for that. He gives to his church persons who have the gift of wisdom (1 Cor. 12:8). Additionally, in response to prayer he gives believers a special portion of wisdom when it is needed and prayed for. James 1:5 says: "If any of you lack wisdom, let him ask of God, that giveth to all men liberally, and upbraideth not; and it shall be given him."

This special gift of wisdom is specifically designed by God to guide his children through the dangerous waters of life in this world. They are mistaken to think they are smart enough to become spiritual men and women through their own reasoning and power.

The world is a dangerous place. Solomon reminds us of this in Ecclesiastes 10:1–2, 8–10:

> Dead flies cause the ointment of the apothecary to send forth a stinking savour: so doth a little folly ruin him that is in reputation for wisdom and honour.
>
> A wise man's heart is at his right hand; but a fool's heart at his left.
>
> He that diggeth a pit shall fall into it; and whoso breaketh an hedge, a serpent shall bite him.
>
> Whoso removeth stones shall be hurt therewith; and he that cleaveth wood shall be endangered thereby.
>
> If the iron be blunt, and he does not whet the edge, then must he put to more strength: but wisdom is profitable to direct.

Solomon addresses the issues of profit in the Book of Ecclesiastes (1:3). He seeks to show how persons may live meaningful and profitable lives. Wisdom alone can provide them with the direction they need. Wisdom alone keeps their hearts focused on duty. Wisdom alone keeps them from doing the one foolish thing that ruins their reputation.

Perfume is of great value, and yet one dead fly added to the mixture spoils the entire batch. It takes a long time to build a good reputation, and no one should underrate its value. However, this valuable possession can be lost forever because of one moment of indiscretion. Wisdom alone allows a person to sharpen the axe of life and avoid the dangers inherent in using a dull axe.

As a college student I worked for the town of South Corning, New York. I left the town shed one morning to clear brush with a dull axe. Within minutes I learned of my folly. I had to work twice as hard as the others, for my axe was dull and theirs were sharp. I worked feverishly to keep up. My greatest danger was outside of my comprehension. The axe, too dull to penetrate, glanced off and went through my boot to the foot beneath. Soon blood was everywhere. I had learned a valuable lesson the hard way. Using a dull axe can be dangerous to one's health.

Two types of wisdom are discussed in the Word of God. One is life giving and the other is unhealthy. James 3:13–18 tells about these two types of wisdom and contrasts them: earthly wisdom and heavenly wisdom. As you examine the characteristics of each, think about yourself and your mate. Are you operating with a dull or a sharp axe? Are you avoiding the pits of the world or stumbling into them?

Wisdom from Below

The wisdom that is from below is based on earthly values. A value is the importance or lack of importance that people attach to the things that surround them. Earthly values are determined by the standards of the world. James states: "This wisdom descendeth not from above, but is earthly, sensual, devilish" (James 3:15). People with earthly values are focused on accumulating wealth or pursuing comfort. They seek power or recognition, rather than how to glorify God (Col. 2:3–4). Their actions parallel those of their father, the devil. This pursuit inevitably creates conflict between people. People with earthly wisdom are characterized also by earthly attitudes. They are consumed with bitter jealousy (James 3:14).

Persons governed by earthly wisdom believe they are always right, and never wrong. This attitude causes much conflict and can destroy intimacy in marriages and other relationships. Marriage requires more give-and-take than other relationships, inasmuch as it requires people to get along twenty-four hours a day.

Pete was a likable guy in many respects. However, he could be abrasive when discussions started. In college we traveled together, and I soon learned that he knew everything. We all knew this to be true, because he reminded us of his superior knowledge daily.

This attitude was hard on his friends and impossible for his family. His argumentative know-it-all style was driving a wedge between him, his friends, and his family. One day his wife confided to my wife that she wasn't sure how much longer she could hang in there. I don't think anything is sadder than selfishness in a husband or wife. Selfishness leads one to look at wives, children and everyone else who comes along as objects to be used. Such sad people hurt everyone around them and ultimately wind up as hollow, reprobate figures.

The wisdom from below produces persons who are driven by selfish ambition. These people always ask, "What's in it for me?" They look out for number one. They are locked into a covenant with self. They maintain a boastful spirit that says, "I'm better than you." This is the heart attitude behind a husband's domineering attitude toward his wife.

The wisdom from below is also seen in the lives of people who have an orientation toward lying. People who lie must win at any cost, representing themselves as something they are not. They do not recognize their behavior as a form of self-deception, encouraged by the "father of lies" (see John 8:44).

People with earthly behavior are also characterized by disorder, in contrast to the natural orderliness that characterizes God's creation (1 Cor. 14:40). Additionally, people with earthly attitudes participate in vile practices. Their time and energies are given to the pursuit of worthless activities that bring them little real progress.

James does not stop with pointing out negative values. He goes on to develop a value system based on "wisdom from above." Those values lead to attitudes and behaviors that please God and nurture relationships.

Wisdom from Above

Wisdom from above generates godly values. Purity is one of the prime characteristics of God. God's children should seek to be morally blameless, free from the taint of evil. God values purity. His children choose to pursue what he values. (1 John 3:3). When we choose to turn our backs on material that enflames illicit passion we are in pursuit of the purity that God values. When we deny our own ambitions and act in the interest of others by feeding or providing for their needs in some tangible way, we are on the path of purity valued by God.

Wisdom from above brings people closer to one another and closer to God (James 3:15–18). It is peace producing. I can remember many times in our marriage when either Peg or I would be irritable. We faced a choice: Should we increase the level of irritability or find a way to lessen it? On such occasions we would remind ourselves of the Bible passage that states: "A soft answer turneth away wrath: but grievous words stir up anger" (Prov. 15:1).

Wisdom from above heals rather than injures. Because the life focus is on giving as opposed to getting, heavenly wisdom thinks of others' needs. When Peg and I focused on meeting one another's needs, the anger between us always dissolved, and peace was restored to our relationship.

Wisdom from above produces a gentle people. In our society the term means softness or weakness. But the Bible's connotation is of people consumed with a desire for "that which is fair and patient." A gentle person knows how to forgive when condemnation would be justifiable. To be gentle is to recognize that, in the long run, relationships between the members of a family are more important than winning or losing some contest sponsored by ego. The higher priority for Christians is people. A compassionate concern over their relationship with God provides the power to consistently be supportive of others.

God places a high value on reasonableness. Reasonable people are willing to listen, willing to be persuaded, and skilled in knowing when to wisely yield. Even the young and inexperienced in life, with heavenly wisdom, can show reasonableness (Prov. 1:4). Being reasonable provides Christians the ability to negotiate with a family member, not storm, "I said it, and that's the way it's going to be!" Reasonableness, to James, implies the ability to admit to being wrong and the willingness to make it right. Solomon counsels godly people to be sensitive to the difference that yielding can make in relationships when he says: "Yielding pacifieth great offenses" (Eccles. 10:4).

Wisdom from above also creates people who are full of mercy and good fruits. This kind of mercy results even when other people have brought the problems on themselves. This mercy offers practical help and manifests a generosity that leads to merciful actions without remuneration (the good Samaritan). In marriage certain circumstances may tempt one to say, "I told you so," or "You made your bed, now lie in it." This smugness is the opposite of what James is talking about. Heavenly wisdom takes into account the hurt and embarrassment already suffered. It does not insist on retaliating. Wisdom from above is manifested in the lives of a people who function without partiality. The unwavering person has settled on values and beliefs by which he charts his life (1 Cor. 15:58). He is steady and operates according to settled absolutes. This characteristic is the opposite of "double mindedness."

Finally, wisdom from above is manifested in the lives of people who function without hypocrisy. These people possess the quality of being real and transparent. They are genuinely concerned about others. I am grateful to God for the privilege of meeting people like this in the churches where I have ministered. I sense they are motivated by a genuine concern for my development and wellbeing. The idea of somehow using me or others to further their own agenda is foreign to their thoughts and motives.

People whose lives are governed by heavenly wisdom are not always appreciated. The world often applauds only those who possess great glamour. However, the people who hold the world together are those who function out of divine wisdom. Without them this world would be unbearably chaotic.

Results of Heavenly Wisdom

"And the harvest of righteousness is sown in peace of them that make peace" (James 3:18). This passage indicates that peace makes right relationships between persons—husbands and wives, parents and children. James summarizes the value system of heavenly wisdom by calling it righteousness. The value system of righteousness results in a set of behaviors he calls sowing in peace by those who make peace. Rightness of behavior is the harvest that comes from the lives of those who have received imputed righteousness through the reception of Christ, who is the wisdom of God as Lord and Savior.

Solomon admonishes believers when he says: "Let thy garments be always white; and let thy head lack no ointment" (Eccles. 9:8). Paul admonishes the Corinthians on the issue of righteousness: "Let us cleanse ourselves from all filthiness of the flesh and spirit, perfecting holiness in the fear of God" (2 Cor. 7:1). To achieve intimacy in marriage, husbands and wives must share a consuming interest in personal holiness. Only then will their marriages be safe and their march toward intimacy be assured a successful completion.

Conclusion

Wisdom is the ability to apply biblical principles creatively to everyday life situations. In this chapter we have distinguished earthly wisdom from heavenly or godly wisdom. As a child of God, you have the potential to be wise, for your source of wisdom, the Lord Jesus Christ, lives within you. His Holy Word, with everything you need to be wise according to God's standards, is available to you.

Growth Exercises

Would you characterize your personal life and marriage relationship as operating out of wisdom from below (false wisdom) or from above (heavenly wisdom)? Right now, are you and your spouse willing to make a commitment to operate out of heavenly wisdom? For a successful marriage, both of you must increasingly learn and apply wisdom's principles and directives to your relationship on a daily basis. Start a walk with wisdom today.

Perhaps you need to receive Christ as your personal Savior so God's wisdom will dwell in you. Are you willing to admit that you are a captive of sin and to receive deliverance through Christ's blood? Ephesians 1:7 says: "In whom we have redemption through his blood, the forgiveness of sin, according to the riches of his grace."

Perhaps you need to repent of sin against your marriage partner and seek his or her forgiveness today. Maybe you are ashamed of your life. Paul says:

"Study to show thyself approved unto God, a workman that needeth not to be ashamed, rightly dividing the word of truth" (2 Tim. 2:15).

The help you need for your marriage is available. Incarnated wisdom—Jesus Christ—and wisdom from the Bible provide what you need to strengthen your marriage. The following exercises will help you focus on some of the important dimensions of divine wisdom and personally apply them to your situation.

1. Begin by together determining the importance of wisdom's direction. Read Ecclesiastes 10, then answer and discuss these questions.

As a result of reading this chapter, would you describe this world as a good or a dangerous place to live in?
According to verse one, how much does it take to ruin a precious or important thing?
If the right hand is the hand of duty, and the left hand is the hand of folly, what would you say verse two means?
In verses 8–10, what kinds of positions do we find humanity in?
What makes it possible to live in such a world?
How important is wisdom to you? To your marriage?

2. Look up and read the texts that show the means by which wisdom is made available. Try to point out to each other where you see manifestations of this wisdom in your own or your spouse's life.

In the Son, Jesus Christ—1 Corinthians 1:30, 31
In the Scriptures, God's Inspired Word—Colossians 3:16, 2 Timothy 3:15
In God's Gifts—James 1:5–8, 1 Corinthians 12:8

3. Read the following passages about how you can improve your relationship through wisdom. Share with each other your answers to these questions.

Read 1 Kings 3:5–14.
What would you ask God for that will help you be the best husband or wife you can possibly be?
Now look specifically at verse seven again. What attitude did Solomon possess that preceded his request for wisdom? How can you exemplify this same attitude in your marriage?

Read Proverbs 4:4–13 Notice, wisdom is personified as a woman. Husbands, God gave you wives as "helpers suitable for you." No one should know you as well as she. Also, she will tell you the truth when no one else will. Therefore, she can become your greatest ally or worst threat. You can gain great wisdom from her if you will allow her to offer loving criticism.

If you treat your spouse as God tells you to treat your guest, what do you think the result would be (according to Prov. 4)?

What can your spouse do to make it easier for you to listen to her or his advice?

Do you ever feel your spouse reacts negatively when you give him or her your opinion? If so, ask what you could do differently that would help her or him to better receive your input.

Additional Reading

2 Timothy 1–4. Note the constant reference to Scripture as Paul counsels young Timothy.

Jay Adams. *Christian Counselors Manual.*

Jay Adams. *More Than Redemption.*

Larry Crabb. *Understanding People.* Grand Rapids: Zondervan, 1987.

Jerry Falwell. *Wisdom for Living.* Wheaton, Ill.: Victor, 1984.

5

Commitment to Reality

Secularists offer a variety of definitions of reality. Existentialists offer the reality that God is dead. Deists ask us to believe that the God who created it all has gone on a permanent vacation. Humanists say that a person doesn't really need God anyway; to them a human being is God, so they emphasize human self-sufficiency, self-determinism, and self-perfectionism. Prosperity theologians try to calm our fears with the idea that "God is a cosmic bellhop." Finally, the New Agers have told us that reality consists of union with God.

True Reality Begins with God

Whom are we to believe and what does all of this have to do with building a stronger marriage? If these views adequately describe reality, not much. However, biblical reality is totally divorced from the conjecturing of these hollow secularists. Biblical reality is the sovereign, loving God working all things together for the good of us, his children, in a world where the things that are wrong are so great in number they cannot be added up, and the crooked seemingly cannot be made straight.

This is the view of reality taught by Solomon and Paul. This is what Solomon said in Ecclesiastes 1:13–15 and 3:11:

This sore travail hath God given to the sons of man to be exercised therewith. I have seen all the works that are done under the sun; and, behold, all is vanity and vexation of spirit. That which is crooked cannot be made straight: and that which is wanting cannot be numbered.

He hath made every thing beautiful in his time: also he hath set the world in their heart, so that no man can find out the work that God maketh from the beginning to the end.

Life is hard. No perfect situations exist, no perfect church, perfect woman, or perfect man. But there is a loving God who strengthens and supports his people, who stands behind all that happens and makes it beautiful for those who love him. If we did not know this and believe it we would easily give up on situations and people. We would feel that every time things get difficult we should run away.

Few have endured such harsh adversity as Joseph (see Gen. 37, 39–40). His father's favorite, he was sold into slavery by his own brothers. A loyal servant in a rich man's household, he was tossed into prison because of a lying accuser. But God used the whole circumstance to save the lives of his chosen family during famine. Joseph recognized this truth (Gen. 50:20).

Joseph hung in there. I am certain he had some bad days. We have bad days in our marriages. We all have times when we feel life is caving in on us. These pressures are a part of our reality. But that is just it; they are only a part of our reality. A comprehensive view of reality sees God standing above the problems and supporting us through them. If we never had problems, we would have a very shallow view of what God can do for his children.

Reality is God with us in difficulties. More than that, it is God carrying us through our difficulties. Remember the story of the man who went to heaven and looked back on the days of his life. He saw footprints on the seashore of his life where Jesus and he had walked together. However, he noticed that during the particularly difficult times only one set of prints was visible. He complained and asked why Jesus had abandoned him during those difficult periods. Jesus replied that he had not abandoned him but carried him. Isn't it wonderful to know that he carries us through the difficult times we experience!

In life we will sometimes be unable to make the crooked straight. We will frequently find that the serious problems in our families or marriages are so great in number they cannot be added up. This reality does not provide us with an excuse to run away. Recognizing that we have come to the end of our limitations only serves to throw us into reliance upon God's enabling and sustaining power. We can remain in difficult situations knowing that God can turn evil to good and make all things beautiful in his time.

Peter reminds us that all Christians are called to some measure of suffering when he says: "For even hereunto were ye called: because Christ also suffered for us, leaving us an example, that ye should follow his steps; . . . when he suffered he threatened not, but committed himself to him that judgeth righteously" (1 Peter 2:21–23).

Speakers who attempt to convince Christians that they are exempt from suffering are deceitful messengers. People who believe their untruthful messages are destined for severe depression or disease; they will lose their energy for building lasting intimacy.

Reality does not begin with human suffering. Reality begins with the God who can turn people's worst intentions to his good purposes. We may not always know the depths of his purpose, but with the eyes of faith we can see the purposefulness of all he brings to pass (Rom. 8:28). The God of the Bible is the only true God, the foundation for all reality.

God plainly presents the content of reality in the Son and in the Scriptures. Our part is to read the record of his Son and his love, believe it, and receive the reality of life through the Holy Spirit. The Word of God is God's means of communicating to people. God is known in the reality of his self-communications concerning himself and his works in his Word. Through the Bible we come to know God, not only as objective fact, but also as loving father, compassionate savior, infinite wisdom and provider of righteousness, redemption, and sanctification. Through these revelations of himself we experience God directly as a person.

Where in the Bible can we find these self-revelations? 2 Timothy 3:16 states that all Scripture is inspired by God. Paul tells us that all of the Bible is given by the Spirit of God. The Bible from cover to cover is the record of God's self-revelation and the effects of that communication on his creation. Paul challenged young Timothy to rightly divide that self-revelation (2 Tim. 2:15). The proper division of God's Word results in bodies of material designed to indoctrinate, reprove, correct, and instruct (2 Tim. 3:16).

A proper response to this material creates husbands and wives who are in a position to grow up. The Scriptures, rightly divided, also produce a spirit of love, power, and sound mindedness in the student of God's Word. What an asset for the couple who desires to move beyond fear to an enjoyment of intimacy! A journey of this type must begin with a personal relationship with Jesus Christ.

The Lord Jesus Christ is the solution to our sin problem; he is the way, the truth, and the life. He is reality, and all reality must be tested against his self-revelation. His self-revelation occurs in the midst of a real world that feels the real effects of sin. Paul speaks of the real world when he writes: "For we know that the whole creation groaneth and travaileth in pain together until now. And not only they, but [we] also . . . groan within ourselves, waiting for the adoption, to wit, the redemption of our body. For we are saved by hope" (Rom. 8:22–24).

There is no greater thrill than finding that the reality of our sin can be covered with the reality of God's self-revelation in Christ. I still remember what it was like to live day after day under the oppressive dominance of sin. What a glorious day when the Holy Spirit entered my life and the reality of my sin was covered with the reality of Christ's blood.

That day would have lost its significance without the ongoing cleansing and enablement that accompanied that invasion. We need power to live with our husbands and wives and maintain a kind and gentle temper. Jesus Christ in our lives is that portion of reality that allows us to serve rather than retreat from our mates. He, through his Spirit, enables us to see Christ in our mates while a myriad of problems have yet to be solved. He fills us with hope—hope generated by faith at work in us.

God exercises his people. Solomon tells us: "I have seen the travail, which God hath given to the sons of men to be exercised in it" (Eccles. 3:10). The world is a vast gymnasium where God faithfully exercises his people to conform them to the image of Christ. Through this lifelong exercise we are brought to maturity in Christ. Our duty is to trust that the one who made us and saved us does have a plan. He has everything under control. God is sovereign. All his exercising is purposeful, good, and beautiful.

In Ecclesiastes 3 we are introduced to the concept that God controls everything we experience in our lives. We may label some times good and some times bad. We may love the time of getting and hate the time of losing. In this passage of Scripture we are told that God makes all of these times beautiful. However, the reality is that we can never determine exactly what God is doing. Faith makes possible our confidence that God makes everything beautiful in his time. God exercises us through his visitation of the times on us.

Exercise is hard work. At one time in my life I loved it. However, I don't mend as quickly as I used to. I still believe exercise is good for me, but it has gotten harder, not easier. Nonetheless, it is good for me. Likewise, I believe that God's exercisings are good. The reality is that sometimes they hurt. Sometimes I cry and confess my inability to withstand the pressures of my personal realities. Only the certain knowledge of God's love based on my understanding of Scripture sustains me.

I am frequently overwhelmed with what the reality of human suffering brings to me. The news just came that a mother shot and killed her three-year-old baby, then turned the gun on herself. This is a powerful part of reality. A dear brother has a terminal brain tumor. A fellow pastor's wife just left him. We could construct a list of tragedies that would fill the rest of this book.

Sorrow is part of reality and serves a useful function in the lives of God's children. Solomon affirms the purposefulness of sorrow when he says, "It is better to go to the house of mourning, than to go to the house of feasting. . . . Sorrow is better than laughter" (Eccles. 7:2–3). Sorrow presents us with a real opportunity for personal growth.

Experience has taught me that the greatest spurts of growth for me often follow times of intense personal struggle. These times of trial produce a sense of personal limitation that causes increased reliance on God. They create a dissatisfaction with the quickly passing luster of this world's charms and point me heavenward to the land of lasting treasures.

In spite of the great benefits to be derived from suffering, God's people dislike this dimension of reality. We quickly get frustrated with the limitations it imposes, and like Paul believe that God will be better served when all thorns are permanently removed from our flesh. When we encounter problems we fall to complaining. We are determined to get the offending reality somehow pushed out of our lives. Little wonder that sometimes we push out of our lives a God who would allow us to suffer.

Suffering is an important part of reality. We must have a good theology of suffering to meet the demands of life. Paul informs us in 2 Corinthians 1 that all suffering is purposeful. Suffering molds moral character. The pain, trials, and difficulties in life provide occasion for us to develop the character to stand tall, live right, walk straight, and be true (exemplified by Job).

Humility is developed in the midst of trials. In the midst of suffering it makes sense to humble ourselves under the hand of God and wait for his timely exaltation (1 Peter 5:6). In such a posture we develop a more congenial, Christ-like personality.

God uses suffering as a wood carver uses a chisel to remove what doesn't belong. I remember attending a fair and watching a wood carver practice his craft. I stood in awe as I observed him. I exclaimed, "How do you do that?" He quietly informed me, "I just see in the block of wood what I want to create and take away what doesn't belong." The chisel carefully removed that which was unnecessary. Frequently that is what God does as he exercises his people (Hos. 6:5). He removes what doesn't belong as he forms Christ in us.

God frequently lays open our real motives for service by visiting us with trials. In the midst of the trials we are to be led along by joy, knowing that all of his actions toward us are grounded in his love (James 1:2). The enlargement and deepening of our personal ministry is developed through suffering. The enablement derived from the experience of suffering permits us to minister to other people more effectively than the most powerful sermon (2 Cor. 1:4).

As a young pastor I once grew very ill. I awakened one morning early and found my heart racing. I was very frightened. I was in the hospital for several days with a rare viral infection whose name defied pronunciation. The doctors calmed me and assured me all would be well in time. They were right, but their words didn't mean as much to me as the words of a brother I had not previously met.

One of the young college students in our church had seen his father suffer from the same infection, and they came to visit me. As the father shared with me and encouraged me, I felt a wonderful calm come over me. He had been where I was and he had survived. He ministered to me in a special way, qualified to do so because he had suffered in exactly the same way I was now suffering. He had been comforted by God (2 Cor. 1) and was now in a position as a part of God's comfort chain to minister to me. God forms comfort chains. We suffer; we receive his comfort; and we are qualified to minister in a special way to those who will suffer as we have.

Now that we understand his program I am sure we will want to volunteer to fill our special place. But the truth is that we will not volunteer. Why? We are afraid. God knows our fears. God forms his comfort chain in spite of our fears concerning personal suffering. This does not explain all human suffering, but it does help us to understand some of God's dealings with us.

Joni is known nationally, not in spite of but because God allowed a dive into shallow water to result in her becoming a paraplegic. Far from being "a useless cripple," she has touched uncounted lives as she yielded her mind and heart to God. Several of her books claim millions of readers.

Many have found Christ to be a real person in the midst of deep trials and sorrow. David Ring has cerebral palsy. His mother and father died when he was young. He was filled with confusion and resentment. In the midst of his suffering he found salvation and a new purpose for living in the reality of Jesus Christ. Now he stands before audiences all over America and proclaims, "I have cerebral palsy. What is your problem?" God uses his crippled body, faltering tongue, and joyful testimony to challenge the hearts of men and women all over this nation. Surely, God's strength is made perfect in weakness and the sufficiency of his grace is discovered (2 Cor. 12:9).

Marriage is hard work. Raising a family is hard work. People who buy into the myth of the "greener grass" won't last the distance. People who retreat from the reality of suffering and struggle will always be looking for the easy place. It is imperative that we courageously deal with the challenges we face in our personal lives and in our marriages. Marriage requires that two persons believe God about sin, salvation, suffering, purpose, and sovereignty. We survive every challenge and march victoriously through personal and marital challenges when we believe God and rely on the enabling power of the Holy Spirit.

Reality Principles Applied to Marriage

1. Two sinners marry, and as males and females they differ physically and psychologically in many important ways. A failure to appreciate these differences often brings them into conflict with one another.

2. Sin has distorted the concept of self and promotes that which is destructive to intimacy in many lives. Sin sponsors selfism and is the enemy of the commitment and companionship which are at the heart of intimacy.

3. God's plan is for the male and female to deal with their sin through Jesus Christ and the power of the Holy Spirit. Then each unique person committed to the other unique person is in a position to build intimacy. God wants each to cooperate with him in the achievement of this fantastic goal. Satan does everything he can to hinder the achievement of that goal.

4. On any given day the number of things lacking in any marriage relationship are so great that they cannot be added up. It helps to stop looking for perfection in the world and to use the Word of God and the power of the Holy Spirit to make marriages the best that they can be. Instead of complaining about our mates,

we need to be committed to the completion of that which is lacking in their lives.

5. Sexual fulfillment is a result of, not a prerequisite for, an intimate relationship.

6. No one can, nor should they try to, meet all of the needs in their partner's life. Some needs only God can meet. This is particularly true when self-esteem and security are the issues. Ultimately each person's value is rooted in a relationship with the Creator who loves, values, and has freely chosen to relate to that person through Jesus Christ.

7. The mistakes of the past cannot be removed from a couple's history. They can forgive them but not forget them. To forgive is to empty the past hurts of their power to damage the relationship in the present. God does this for his people through Christ's blood. Through confession and cleansing God removes the power of condemnation from past sins. They can no longer stand over against us, condemn us, and becloud our fellowship with God. God asks that we do with the sins of others against us what he has done with our sins against him. Intimacy is impossible without forgiveness.

Conclusion

Reality is not pretty. It brings God's people into contact with loss, temptation, injustice, and a host of other unpleasant experiences. Believers are involved in spiritual warfare, and Satan is committed to the destruction of every godly marriage. However, regardless of the problems, God's rich and inexhaustible resources are sufficient to carry us through.

God frequently exercises our faith through trials and sorrows. The time of losing is as beautiful in the divine plan as the time of getting. It's all part of our reality. Is there an area of your reality that you have been unhappy with? Why not let God be God? Thank him sincerely for all the things that are happening in your life. You will never be free to move into intimacy with God or your mate if your life is filled with grumbling and complaining against him. Intimacy is impossible without trust and forgiveness and a commitment to completing that which is lacking in the lives of our loved ones.

Growth Exercises

1. In the Book of Ecclesiastes Solomon offers the following observation on life: "And I gave my heart to seek and search out by wisdom concerning all things that are done under heaven; this sore travail hath God given to the sons of man to be exercised therewith. I have seen all the works that are done under the sun; and behold, all is vanity and vexation of spirit. That which is crooked cannot be made straight: and that which is wanting cannot be numbered" (1:13–15).

   Together look at how the statements in this passage describe the realities of your marriage.

   > You may seek to understand through wisdom all the things that are going on in your marriage and family.
   > This task, frequently grievous, is given by God to you as a couple to exercise you.
   > Seeking to understand everything is like grasping for the wind.
   > The crooked often cannot be made straight, and the things that are wrong in any given situation (including your marriage) cannot be numbered. Make a list of some things that are going on in your family and marriage that are vigorously exercising you.

   Read Ecclesiastes 2. In the midst of numberless problems, what is the personal response that Solomon gives? I call this a frustration response to the realities of life. Can you identify this frustration response? Is there another way to handle these problems? In the midst of all these numberless problems, what does Solomon believe God is doing, according to Ecclesiastes 3:1–11? I call this a faith response to the realities that trouble believers. Is this your response?

   Paul affirms the same truth in Romans 8:28. Read it. The reality of our lives is that we all are touched by suffering and loss since we live in a world where the number of things wrong in any situation cannot be added up. What does this mean personally to you as you think about your marriage?

Suffering is only half of the believer's reality. Above the suffering is the sovereign God who makes all things beautiful and good in his time. Joseph recorded his recognition of this truth in Genesis 50:20. What does this other half of reality mean to you as you think of your personal life and marriage?

2. Examine the following statements. Choose your response to each one, a yes if you agree or a no for disagreement with the statement. Where possible, explain to your spouse why you answered with yes or no. Honesty may be painful, but the more open you are with each other the more progress you will make toward intimacy.

Christians don't have marriage problems.
God can miraculously heal our marriage.
Submission means denial of my feelings and ideas.
A good marriage means no fights.
Loneliness is cured by marriage.
Children help a marriage.
I can change my mate.
I can meet all my mate's needs.
Good sex means a good marriage.
Men and women are too different to really understand each other.
Faith in God has nothing to do with a strong marriage.
Friends are just as important to me as my mate.
Romance is essential for a good marriage.
Marriage is better when someone is clearly in charge.

Additional Reading

Pat Springle. *Codependency.* Houston: Rapha Publishing/ Word, 1990.

Chuck Swindoll. *Living on the Ragged Edge.* Waco: Word, 1985.

Warren Wiersbe. *Classic Sermons on Suffering.* Grand Rapids: Kregel, 1984.

6

Commitment to God's Sovereignty

You have read the title of this chapter and are wondering why in the world a discussion of God's sovereignty is included in a book on strengthening marriages. You thought such a discussion was reserved for sermons on theology.

Someone has said, "According to your concept of God, you will live and work." Think about that. You, as a couple and as individuals, will live and work according to the way you view God. Is he a big God? Is he limited? Do you believe he is in control of every detail of your life?

You need to ask God to broaden your concept of him so you can see and know him as he really is. You need to be committed to reality, but reality is terrifying without faith in the sovereign God. The doctrine of divine sovereignty gives meaning and substance to all the other doctrines of the Bible. This chapter will develop the concept of God's sovereignty and its relationship to the believer's life.

Discussions of God's sovereignty must be related to discussions of God's character. It is one thing to have a God who is all powerful and in absolute control of all that comes to pass. It is another matter to believe in a God who uses all that power consistently for the benefit of his people. Believers affirm faith in a God who is too loving to be unkind and too wise to make a mistake, who in pledging his love pledges that he will constantly work all things together for their personal good.

It is important not to misunderstand this divine pledge. God has not pledged himself to support your comfort. He is not a "cosmic bellhop." He has pledged the investment of his energies for the meeting of your needs but not for the provision of your every desire.

God's ultimate concern is to provide you with those things that will help you to become like Jesus Christ. This is ultimately the best goal you could pursue. He has also pledged himself to equip you with those things you need for the maintenance of your lives while you carry out your ministry for his glory. True, he frequently allows you to accumulate more things than you need, but that is not what he has pledged. Sometimes the extras are entrusted to your care to use them for the good of others. Sometimes the extras are the result of your operating from a set of values that are really not in step with God's best plan for you. Those things are acquired through extra hours earning extra dollars, and frequently, they take a big toll on family relationships.

A young doctor friend of mine has just moved into a new million-dollar house. He has to work extra hours to make the mortgage payments. He confided, "I wish I had never bought this place. It's a millstone around my neck. I have no time with the family now."

The sovereignty of God is a source of invaluable inspiration for God's children. The sovereign God has absolute authority and rule over his creation. There are no accidents in a believer's life. Many difficult situations may emerge as they journey through life. However, God is the almighty one, the possessor of all power in heaven and earth, and no power in heaven or earth can thwart his plans or resist his will. The psalmist understood this well and stated, "But our God is in the heavens: he hath done whatsoever he hath pleased" (Ps. 115:3).

Husbands and wives who do not understand God's sovereignty believe in a God who is too small to sustain them through the trials of life. This belief in a small god will leave its adherents cowering in anxious fear before the ups and downs and challenges of marriage. It will rob men and women of sound mindedness and a spirit of power (2 Tim. 1:7). It will rob husbands and wives of their ability to rest in the Lord and wait confidently on him for answers to the problems that come to everyone. Henry F. Lyte, writer of "Abide with Me," voiced the security and peace that the child of God knows in a constantly changing world:

> Change and decay
> In all around I see.
> O thou who changest not,
> Abide with me.

Joy is of great importance in marriages. The partners' joyful support of one another is imperative. 1 John 1:4 reads: "These things write we unto you, that your joy may be full." Why is joy so important? In Nehemiah 8:10 is the answer: "For the joy of the Lord is your strength."

Marriage partners need all the strength they can find. A firm belief in God's control over all the circumstances of life causes them to be overwhelmed with joy. This joy is the key to their strength as persons. It provides them with the strength they need to be godly husbands, wives, and parents.

To say that God is sovereign is to affirm that his right is the right of the potter over the clay, that he may mold that clay into whatever form he chooses. Jeremiah 18:3–6 contains these powerful words:

> Then I went down to the potter's house, and, behold, he wrought a work on the wheels. And the vessel that he made of clay was marred in the hand of the potter: so he made it again another vessel, as seemed good to the potter to make it. Then the word of the Lord came to me, saying, O house of Israel, cannot I do with you as this potter? saith the Lord.

God has absolute and indisputable rights over his creation. He holds sovereign power to implement his designs. This reality allowed Solomon to say, "To everything there is a season, and a time to every purpose under the heaven" (Eccles. 3:1). Paul shared this conviction. The God he worshiped works all things according to his purpose (Rom. 8:28).

Amazingly, believers are easily unsettled by circumstances. I recently talked with a man who would soon turn forty. He was in a state of panic. His life was over, so he thought. Isn't that tragic? God's sovereignty easily extends to his ability to make all Christians his powerful servants regardless of their age. No matter what the circumstances, they can rely on the enablement that is theirs through his mighty power.

Some of God's children may, like Joseph, spend years in Egypt. Some may dwell in seeming obscurity, but God never forgets them and knows exactly where they are. In his time he calls them forth to fulfill his purpose. They may rest in the certain hope that since they are never out of his hand they are forever on the edge of their greatest hours of service. This hopefulness transforms them and infuses their relationships with power. The value of that power for the establishment of intimacy in the marital relationship cannot be overestimated.

The Value of the Doctrine of Sovereignty

A belief in divine sovereignty deepens our worship of God so we do not question his purpose. We bow before him in an attitude of reverent submission, recognizing that our very existence is through him. Paul summarized this thought well in 1 Corinthians 8:6 when he said, "But to us there is but one God, the Father, of whom are all things, and we in him; and one Lord Jesus Christ, by whom are all things, and we by him." Husbands and wives who believe this are possessed of a humility that makes them teachable and divorces them from independent attitudes that destroy intimacy.

A belief in divine sovereignty affords a sense of absolute security. God is infinite in power, so then "I will not fear: what can man do unto me" (Ps. 118:6)? "What time I am afraid, I will trust in thee" (Ps. 56:3). "I will both lay me down in peace, and sleep: for thou, Lord, only makest me dwell in safety" (Ps. 4:8).

People who believe these things are a stabilizing element wherever they go. The husband or wife who carries these convictions into relationships is going to engender a sense of calmness and peacefulness. The dishwasher may break down, the money may not go far enough, but it's okay. God is their security. Intimacy is possible and desirable with such persons.

A belief in divine sovereignty supplies comfort in sorrow and trials. Afflictions are not by chance but are ordained by God (1 Thess. 3:3; 1 Peter 1:6, 7). The psalmist said, "If I take the wings of the morning, and dwell in the uttermost parts of the sea; even there shall thy hand lead me, and thy right hand shall hold me" (Ps. 139:9–10).

The great evangelist Charles H. Spurgeon in his sermon on Matthew 20:15 said, "There is no attribute more comforting to His children than that of God's sovereignty. Under the most adverse circumstances, in the most severe trials, they believe that sovereignty has ordained their afflictions, that sovereignty over-rules them and that sovereignty will sanctify them all."

The power for good in such a conviction cannot be overestimated. James told Christians to count it all joy when they underwent trials. How is such an attitude possible? It is possible when they truly believe in divine sovereignty. Consider the calmness that such a view produces in the minds and actions of those who believe it wholeheartedly. Listen to the apostle Paul when he says, "For I am persuaded" (Rom. 8:38–39). Listen to the psalmist when he exclaims, "This is the day which the LORD hath made; we will rejoice and be glad in it" (Ps. 118:24). The ability to maintain inner calm or joy is rooted in the psalmist's conviction that God is sovereign. It is God who has given the day as a gift to his children. God's sovereignty extends to his control over the sequences of those days.

Solomon grasps this principle fully when he states that the day of joy and the day of weeping are alike, beautiful because they are given sequentially by the sovereign God who has in mind purposes he wishes to effect in his children's lives. We must believe in his sequencing or we will be robbed of joy. It is a matter of utmost importance that Christians be optimistic about God's gift of the days as we receive them. We can never afford to believe that God's arrangement of these days is anything less than purposeful. What could bring greater blessing to a marital relationship than the calm which comes through belief in God's sovereignty?

Couples I see for counseling are usually anything but calm. They are in turmoil and complaining vigorously about the problems they have experienced. How calm they become when they learn to celebrate the difficult times as divine gifts and realize that what they label good and bad are all beautiful gifts from the sovereign God. Without inner calmness intimacy of spirit, soul, and body are impossible. The use of the terms *joy* and *gladness* in Psalm 118 is interesting. Rejoicing has to do with an outer sense of expectation over the gift of the day. Gladness in the Hebrew language refers to an inner sense of calmness and confidence. The outer excitement has been turned inward, and the knowledge of God's control produces an inner calm and sense of personal well-being. How wonderful to have as a partner a person who demonstrates both outer excitement and inner tranquility rooted in the almighty God.

A belief in divine sovereignty puts to death the "victim mentality." Belief in God's sovereignty brings with it the confession that he is Lord over every event a Christian experiences. His plan for each life is personal and loving and includes the maximum use of each person's gifts for his glory. Nothing happens by chance; God does everything for the Christian's best. There are no victims. A victim is someone who was in an accident that serves no beneficial purpose. No such events occur in the life of the believer who is under the hand of the sovereign God.

Joe and Mabel were devastated when their first baby died of pneumonia. A kindly pastor explained God's love and told them they now had a child in heaven. Desiring to be reunited with their child one day, they accepted God's gift of salvation and spent their lives in active Christian service.

Saints in prisons or concentration camps have endured "as seeing him." In Nepal, Prem Prahdan's jailer heard him talking aloud. No one had been put with him in the filthy crawl-in corner where dead bodies had been stored. "Who is in there with you?" bawled the jailer. Prem answered, "Jesus. He's with me everywhere I go."

Victims are depressed and angry. They are not very attractive people to be with. Intimacy with them is not something to be desired. Saying yes to God's sovereignty means they must say no to any tendency to think of themselves as victims. Experiences of the past may have hurt deeply, but God can take them all in his hands and transform them into opportunities for unique and fruitful ministry. Paul shared this truth with the Corinthian believers. He said, "Blessed be God, even the Father of our Lord Jesus Christ, the Father of mercies, and the God of all comfort; who comforteth us in all our tribulation, that we may be able to comfort them which are in any trouble, by the comfort where- with we ourselves are comforted by God" (2 Cor. 1:3, 4).

God in his sovereignty is forging a comfort chain. Every prob- lem known to man is experienced by God's children. God fills them with his comfort and commissions them to minister to oth- ers who suffer as they have. These believers, chosen for suffer- ing, are uniquely prepared to offer a ministry of comfort.

A belief in divine sovereignty enables Christians to be submis- sive to him. We can never surrender our scheming initiative to anyone less than the sovereign God. All personal schemes are calculated to produce self-protection and can be surrendered only when Christians are convinced that the God who is more inter- ested in the individual's benefit than we are has committed all his resources to our protection and advancement. Additionally, Christians must be convinced that this God, to whom they sub- mit, has all power and can never be deterred from accomplishing his purposes. The sovereign God of Scripture meets both of these criteria.

To bow before this God is one of the secrets of peace and hap- piness. Persons who experience such peace make good marriage partners. They are capable of a level of intimacy that those devoid of personal peace can only dream of.

Solomon on Reality and Sovereignty

We have already discussed Solomon's view of reality. In the Book of Ecclesiastes he maintains that life is full of problems. Regardless of a person's situation on this planet, the wrong things are too numerous to be added up (Eccles. 1:15). However, all problems are answered by a Christian's belief in divine sovereignty. God makes everything beautiful in his time. No one can comprehend the mystery of his dealings with people. They can only bow before him in the certain knowledge that he who controls all things is completely for them (Eccles. 3:11–14).

Solomon maintains that life is vain (Eccles. 1:2). Solomon uses the term to describe life's emptiness for persons cut off from divine wisdom. Such persons cannot find profit. They can discover nothing in their world that fills life with meaning and purpose. Wisdom alone gives direction to such persons, for "wisdom is profitable to direct" (Eccles. 10:10).

Ultimately, the sovereign God visited the human family and said, "I am the way, the truth, and the life" (John 14:6). Wisdom directs people to "live joyfully with the wife whom thou lovest" (Eccles. 9:9). In him we have divine wisdom (1 Cor. 1:30). We have direction, purpose, and power for intimacy that transcends anything the hollow persons of this world can conceive.

Conclusion

The knowledge of God's sovereignty produces inward stability and composure. The value of these personal characteristics for the enrichment of your relationship as a married couple is beyond estimation. Resting in his sovereignty you can commit yourselves totally to his care. Have you as a couple presented yourselves as living sacrifices to God? Paul begs believers to make this commitment (Rom. 12:1, 2).

Perhaps you can point back to the time when you made that love gift to God. But the problem with "living sacrifices" is that they have the tendency to jump off the altar. Therefore it is important to be "crucified with Christ" every day, to "put to death the works of the flesh." Will you commit yourself to staying on the altar? Will you stop struggling with God and be that clay in the potter's hand, pliable and moldable? Will you commit yourself to resting in God's sovereignty?

Growth Exercises

1. Read the following passages and answer the questions together.
     Genesis 50:15–21. Why was Joseph able to forgive his brothers after they had attempted to totally ruin his life?

Ecclesiastes 3:10–11. What does God want to accomplish in every circumstance? When does he want to do that?

Romans 8:28–29. What is the promise given here by God? What is the only condition you must meet to claim that promise?

2 Corinthians 1:3–5. What two characteristics are ascribed to God here? What is God's purpose in allowing you to go through difficulty?

2 Corinthians 12:7–10. Why did God allow Satan to trouble Paul with a "thorn"? What was God's answer when Paul fervently asked God to take it away?

Job 42:1–6. Throughout this book Job stated clearly that he felt God had treated him unfairly. After God spoke to him and showed him God's majesty and power, what was Job's response?

What do all of these passages mean to you?

What effect would it have in your relationship with your husband/wife if you did not believe what Joseph believed about himself and his situation?

What effect will believing what Joseph believed about himself and his situation have on you and your relationship with your partner?

2. Examine the following verses and identify their meanings for each of you.

1 Timothy 6:11–21 tells who God is. What does Paul believe about Jesus Christ, according to verses 15 and 16?

In Psalm 139:13–16 what does David say he believes about God's sovereignty and its application to who he is as a person? To what extent and in what ways did God determine David's personality?

3. How would not believing in God's sovereignty affect you as a person? What would be the impact of belief in God's sovereignty on you? How would that belief or disbelief impact your relationship with your partner? Each of you write out an answer and discuss your responses.

Additional Reading

J. I. Packer. *Knowing God*. Downers Grove: InterVarsity, 1973.

F. A. Schaeffer. *The God Who Is There*. Downers Grove: InterVarsity, 1968.

A. W. Tozer. *The Pursuit of God*. Harrisburg, Penn.: Christian Publications, 1955.

7

Commitment to the Other Person

No doubt your wedding day is a wonderful memory for you. Perhaps from time to time you get your pictures out and reminisce. As you look at the smiling faces you can still remember the joyful expectations that filled your mind and heart.

As time went by, and you became better acquainted with that other person in the pictures, you were faced with a sobering reality: the person sitting across from you at the dinner table was very different from the one you thought was standing next to you at the altar. Sometimes the differences have been overwhelming, and you have felt betrayed and angry. What do you do? Do you get rid of the person? Unfortunately, that route is often taken.

There is, however, an alternative to divorce. You can gain a better understanding of the person you are married to. Armed with that understanding and a commitment to your spouse you may participate in the transformation of your marriage.

In this chapter I discuss commitment between marriage partners. I examine some principles you can use in your quest for deepening your marriage relationship. The logical place to begin is with the person you married. Who is he or she? First you must wholeheartedly acknowledge him or her as a person.

Understanding the Other Person Is Crucial

You married a real person. Your spouse has some real strengths and some real weaknesses, as well as some glaring problems. Everyone does. But good marriages from the beginning are built on a firm foundation of commitment. You need wholeheartedly to pledge your energies to assist God with the task of transforming you and the person he has given you. Frequently people marry those who are very different from themselves. This can be very good if one is strong in areas where the other is weak. However, we often focus on these differences and find in them sources of aggravation.

I am naturally outgoing and verbal. Peg is more quiet and not as gifted in public speaking as I am. I will never forget the time I volunteered her to speak to a group in a church where I was holding meetings. I had not checked with her and did not inform her that she was speaking until we arrived. She was upset and spent the night preparing her topic. I could have prepared in an hour. Before long we both were upset. Can you imagine that? I was doing a marriage enrichment seminar, and we were fighting.

I asked her forgiveness for trying to make my strength her strength. I was not honoring her and living within her limitations. I expected her to do that for me, but I was not doing it for her. She forgave me. I don't plan to make that mistake again.

It takes conscious effort to understand your spouse. You must appreciate the physical, intellectual, emotional, volitional, and spiritual dimensions of his or her personality.

People as Body

She was only twenty-four when the doctors gave her the news. She had diabetes. Her husband promised to help her with the new challenge in her life. They were not prepared for the temper tantrums, near-coma experiences, and depressive episodes they would have to share. We all live in bodies that are to a greater or lesser degree affected by Adam's fall. Paul summarized the problem well when he stated, "We ourselves groan within ourselves, waiting for the adoption, to wit, the redemption of our body" (Rom. 8:23).

The body is a complex biochemical organism. When all is working well, it is a source of wonderment and pleasure. When it malfunctions, the list of potential problems is overwhelming and somewhat frightening. Some of these problems people bring on themselves. They are the result of poor stewardship. Poor nutrition, poor sleeping habits, lack of exercise, abuse of foreign substances (drugs, alcohol, caffeine) and a host of other bad habits contribute to the generation of serious problems for humans. A dysfunctional body presents great obstacles to the achievement of intimacy. A sound body is a great blessing. All reasonable efforts should be made to insure that our bodies are functioning at their optimal potential.

Christians must be good stewards of their bodies for two reasons. First, their bodies are temples of the Holy Spirit (1 Cor. 6:19). The Holy Spirit should not have to dwell in a body whose usefulness is blunted by a sinful lack of self-discipline. Christians honor him when they care for their bodies. Second, Christians' bodies are their major instruments for ministry. They meet the needs of others and participate in their assigned missions in their bodies. The better the condition of their bodies the more stamina and energy they can bring to their ministries and marriages.

All consideration for beauty and charm aside, Christians must face God's Word: "Ye are not your own." They have no room to say, "What I eat, smoke, and put in my body is nobody's affair but mine." It is God's dwelling place they are caring for or abusing.

More often than not, when one spouse quietly sets an example of excellence in any area, the other will adopt that pattern. One (who *may not* even be the one who most needs the change) begins to cut back on the junk food. Soon less flab and more energy are evident. For that reason, if nothing else, the other may join the effort. Whatever the reason, the result is the same: a healthier, more alive, more attractive person.

Everyone should make the most of what they have. Good stewardship of bodies pays healthy dividends in the area of physical intimacy. Couples need to maintain an effort to be physically attractive for one another. That does not mean that the wife must always be "model thin." Women are under a lot of cultural pressure where the issue of weight is concerned. Men can have "donelaps disease" (stomach done lapped over the belt) and it's all right, but women gain a little extra and they are considered unattractive. This kind of reasoning is one of the finely honed premises that flow from the satanic wedge and does great damage to a couple's ability to achieve physical intimacy. Nevertheless, feeling well and feeling attractive helps both men and women to be more attractive.

People as Soul

Genesis speaks clearly to the issue of man's creation: "And the LORD God formed man of the dust of the ground, and breathed into his nostrils the breath of life; and man became a living soul (Gen. 2:7). What a paradox! Man is a combination of dirt and divine breath. Little wonder he has been capable of such great good and tragic evil.

The term *soul* is a complex one. Generally it designates the immaterial dimension of human life. I understand the term to be a synonym for the intellectual, emotional, and volitional dimensions of humanness.

Intellectual processes are somewhat unique to each individual. Mental abilities are products of nature (the genetic stuff) and nurture (knowledge gained or lost through the quality of the learning environment). This general inheritance may be strengthened or weakened by what the mind is "fed," which explains why the Bible places such great emphasis on people's responsibility to take care of their minds (Prov. 23:7).

Men and women generally think differently in many important ways. Women tend to think, "Whom will this affect and how?" Men tend to think in terms of "What will this do?" and to be more concerned about the short term. Women tend to think more about the long-range impact of what is being proposed. Together they make a great team.

Blending your various thought patterns, accepting your varying levels of intelligence, and appreciating the intelligence of each other in different areas (such as verbal and performance) is indeed intelligent. Failure to appreciate your mate's intellectual contribution to the welfare of the team is the ultimate put-down. Intimacy will be impossible in such a situation.

A story, which may sound familiar, points out the difference in the ways husbands and wives sometimes approach tasks. A couple were going shopping. The husband asked the wife, "What are we shopping for?" She replied, "A dress." On arriving at the store he went straight for the dress rack. She, on the other hand, made her way to the dress rack by browsing through the housewares, shoes, school supplies, and cosmetics. She was shopping, he was hunting.

Achieving intimacy in marriage is impossible if you do not appreciate the relative strengths of the male and female approaches to solving problems. Peg saves us hundreds of dollars a year with her approach to shopping. I waste hundreds of dollars a year with mine. She watches for values and shops ahead. I wait until my need is critical and pay full price. Her conservative and cautious approach to spending is sometimes aggravating, but I have learned that this is one of her unique ways of contributing to the strengthening of our team. I now tolerate the behavior better because I see its value. Her way of shopping is only one of the hundreds of ways her reasoning processes strengthen our marriage.

On the other hand, I like to come to closure on things. This is sometimes a real strength in our relationship. She can have difficulty at times bringing something to a conclusion. For several years we looked for land on which to build a house. She may get five projects started simultaneously, then not finish any of them. I sometimes need to step in and bring things to closure. Again, we balance each other. The balance creates a sense of appreciation. The appreciation deepens our intimacy.

Humans are also deeply emotional. They can repress their feelings or let them flow freely. Regardless of which way they go, emotions are intensely real and important to everyone.

When people repress their true feelings, they may come out in unpredictable ways or in unexpected places. When they let their emotions run wild they have a hard time building lasting relationships.

Thoughts affect emotions. Positive thoughts generally produce positive feelings. If feeling good is your goal, then it is important that you fill your mind with good things. Thinking is really the central issue to consider if you wish to overcome bad feelings. Thinking, feeling, and acting are closely related behaviors in humans. If you think positively and act out of those positive thoughts, then good feelings will almost always follow. The only exception to this pattern is the person who has some type of organic or biochemical problem.

Emotions are important for the achievement of intimacy. It is important that husbands and wives feel safe and comfortable expressing emotions to each other. This does not mean they will tell each other everything. Critical thoughts hurt only the thinker if left unsaid; unspoken, they may smolder in a heart forever. A word is not dead when it is said. On the contrary, it just begins to live.

I love sharing my feelings with Peg. It helps tremendously just to know that I have a safe place where I can do that. However, I have learned the hard way that some emotion sharing has a negative impact on intimacy. If my feelings are the result of critical thinking, sharing them may only serve to make her feel sad.

I now try not to share feelings freely if I realize that I just want to get something off my mind. I ask myself whether the feeling will make her sad. If the sharing will make her sad and no apparent good can be derived from her sadness, then I don't share the feeling with her. I share it with God or with a trusted counselor. My objective in sharing my feelings with her is to build intimacy, not tear it down. One of my personal prayers is that the Holy Spirit will make me sensitive to the difference.

Another dimension of soul life is the will (Hos. 5:11). A combination of thoughts and emotions pushes you to behave in a certain way. However, God has created you with the ability to choose and he holds you responsible for your choices. There is a sense in which you are free in the area of choice. This freedom can wonderfully enhance intimacy or destroy it.

You as a free person will yourself into a committed relationship with another person. This is exciting. You have chosen her or him. The value of such a choice for strengthening intimacy is unparalleled. You are not in this relationship because you have to be; you are in it because you want to be with every fiber of your being. You have willed it. Intimacy flourishes when supported by such a free choice.

People as Spiritual

A matter of great importance is that you bring your bodies, minds, emotions, and wills under the control of the Holy Spirit. The unregenerated soul life of humans is in rebellion against God. Your relationship with God affects our relationships with each other. God has designed you with a need for a relationship with him. If that relationship is not in place, then the physical, intellectual, emotional, and volitional elements of our lives will serve only to hinder us in our search for intimacy. Each of these areas will be imprisoned by sin, and the energy of these areas will be focused on self-satisfaction.

John is not a Christian. He came to me for help with saving his marriage. He confessed that when he was in high school, girls did not pay much attention to him. Now that he is out of high school and working, things are different. He states, "I can have any woman I want." His money is spent on going out, buying things, and "just getting along."

John is in prison. He appears free but he is a prisoner of sin. His psychological needs demand that he arrange all of his resources to prove that he is now a person of value. Everyone and everything around him is merely a resource to achieve that end.

Sue is John's wife. She professes to be a Christian but has given no consideration to the spiritual dimension of the battle between her and John. She keeps hoping that maybe he will change. A failure to understand the spiritual dimensions of the problem and the requisite need of God's intervention for resolution make the achievement of intimacy impossible for John and Sue. Until John understands his need for deliverance through Jesus Christ, and Sue appreciates the need for walking with God, the two can only go from tragedy to tragedy.

You must constantly stay in God's Word if you hope to maintain spiritual vibrancy in yourselves and in your marital rela-

tionship. The sinful flesh constantly rises up and makes demands
that, if filled, will do immeasurable damage to intimacy. You must
reckon yourselves dead to such demands and provide the Holy
Spirit with what he needs to dwell in you in fullness of power
(Gal. 2:20, Eph. 5:18–33, Col. 3:12–25). Spiritual power is important in the strengthening of marital intimacy. It creates an energy
within the individual to deal with the selfism that undermines
and destroys true intimacy.

Acceptance Is Crucial

Understanding the person you are married to is important.
Next to understanding him or her, acceptance is the foundation
for all interpersonal relationships. Accepting her means loving
her in spite of what she thinks, feels, or does. Accepting him does
not mean that you have to be in agreement with his thoughts,
feelings, or actions. You may disagree with an action while still
maintaining love and acceptance of the person. Your human tendency is to reject the person for qualities you dislike or for actions
with which you disagree.

Mary had just discovered her husband was sexually abusing
their fourteen-year-old daughter. He was unrepentant and blamed
the daughter because, he maintained, "She is sexually provocative
around the house." He refused to take steps to insure the daughter's protection, such as putting locks on the inside of her bedroom door.

Mary said, "I love you, but you will not live in this house until
you are willing to seek counseling and deal with your sin." Mary
had followed a difficult path. She was implementing real love.
She did not reject her husband but let him know that until he
met certain conditions she would not reconcile. He never did
meet those conditions, and she had to separate from him.

Intimacy is not possible unless you acknowledge and accept
your differences. Each partner brings into the marriage different habits, values, temperaments, and tastes. Even a graduate
degree in psychology cannot protect you from the hard work that
awaits you after the wedding. The individual idiosyncracies that

must be endured and dealt with after marriage constitute a real challenge.

There is no one in the whole world exactly like him or her. Everyone has a unique personality, with a large percentage of it being formed by six years of age. Everyone has come through many experiences that have dramatically affected thought patterns, emotions, and responses to things around them and that makes them unique. Much of what makes your spouse what he or she is you had nothing to do with. You can only accept and work with him. The process of transformation commences when the Holy Spirit brings the need for change to his attention. You can help with the process of change, but if you try to play Holy Spirit you may do great damage to the intimacy level in your relationship.

Paul would not accept John Mark (Acts 15:36–40). So Barnabas discipled the young man. The result of Barnabas' acceptance and investment in John Mark was the development of a young man who became valuable to Paul and the church of Jesus Christ. While closing his letter to Timothy, Paul said: "Take Mark, and bring him with thee: for he is profitable to me for the ministry" (2 Tim. 4:11). Acceptance and investment made the difference. Paul understood this, and his relationship with young Timothy was enriched by the dual strengths of acceptance and investment.

Adaptation Is Crucial

We are never exactly as others would like us to be. Have you noticed how that frequently becomes an excuse for breaking off a relationship? John reports that he is no longer Steve's friend, because "he wasn't what I thought he was." Sometimes that is a valid reason for breaking away. However, often such words portray a shallowness in understanding relationship building.

It is important that marriage partners affirm each other for who they are and begin to adapt to each other. When a couple can appreciate their differences and adapt to meeting one another's needs within the context of those differences, intimacy can thrive. They have given each other space for separateness while still adapting and strengthening oneness.

Recently Peg left for a three-day visit with her parents in New York State. Ten minutes after she went out of the driveway I missed her. It was important that she go. She was to see a cousin, home from the mission field after twenty years. She needed to visit her parents. She needed the rest and relaxation. I was happy for her. I was glad that I could help provide some of the means by which she could take the break. She does it for me all the time. Often when I am down she adapts and gets up. We have consciously practiced adaptation. It is good for intimacy; it speaks of concern for each other that is greater than selfism; it creates an environment for the ultimate growth of both partners.

The survival of intimacy demands a successive series of adaptations that rest on a foundation of sensitivity. You must listen to the heart of your mate and seek to discover where she is in her struggle with the challenges of life. How are you both doing with your feelings about yourselves? What's happening to self-esteem now that the children are taking up all your time, or are up and away? What is she thinking today? What is he feeling? Does she need a stronger sense of self? Does he? How can you reallocate your time and resources to make your oneness, or your separateness, more satisfying?

Is something in the way of this adaptation, something on which you place more value? Sam sat where he always sat during football season; his eyes were glued to the television. Janet had taken all she could. She stood directly between Sam and the television and said, "I've got to know! Do you love me more than football?" Sam looked at her face and knew he was in trouble. Thoughtfully he replied, "Well . . . I love you more than baseball." Sam had missed the point. He's not alone. Many have missed the point at one time or another in their marriages.

People let idols come into their lives. Sports, education, jobs, and a host of other activities capture their energies. It's easy to forget the implicit pledge in the wedding vows to focus time and energy on the building of an intimate relationship with a spouse. Sam was stealing from Janet. He was taking energy that by right belonged to her and sharing it with a prostitute named football.

You need to invest energy in your partner. You need to know where she is in thought, feeling, spirit, and body. Then in humble submission you need to make it your goal to make her the strongest servant of Christ she can possibly become. You need to adapt your schedule, energies, and resources to guarantee the successful achievement of that goal. Adaptation to make another strong is the job of a servant. Good mates are good servants. Serving will generate intimacy.

Appreciation Is Crucial

I like being appreciated. In fact, I have difficulty sustaining long-term relationships when I feel unappreciated. I don't think I'm alone in this. When it comes to strengthening intimacy in marriage, appreciation is crucial. Showing and expressing appreciation for the unique individual I am married to is a key to my successful marriage.

I am not just talking about appreciating people for what they contribute to relationships. That is important. However, beyond appreciation for what they do is their need to be appreciated for what they are as individuals. Inside each is awareness of the fact that they cannot always perform successfully. This reality creates the need for a relationship where even if they fail they will be valued and appreciated.

Appreciation for the other person should go beyond appreciation of physical appearance. Complimenting another on the physical can be important, but at the center of the compliment should be the real person. Instead of saying, "I love that dress," try, "I love that dress on you." More than anything else, a person needs to hear from a mate, "I love being with you."

Here are a number of practical ways you can show your mate you appreciate him or her.

Say thank you.
Offer direct words of appreciation for
    taking care of their appearance.
    a job well done.
    being genuine.
Compliment them for
    the way they handle difficult situations.

their faithfulness with the details of caring for jobs, home,
   family.
shielding you from unpleasant phone calls.
their patience with you.
Patiently listen and withhold interrupting comments and judg-
   ment until they have finished what they want to tell you.
Show you value them enough to create an island of safety
   where they can
      cry.
      show their weaknesses (within reason).
      confess their faults.
      be unconditionally loved.
      be encouraged during times of discouragement.
      dream their dreams.
Be loyal.

A wife recently said, "My husband is such a great guy. He
probably sees my faults more clearly than I do. But I know
he is always *for* me, never against me. He gives me security and the room I need for personal growth." The loyal
person never cuts the partner down. The loyal person
avoids situations of temptation with members of the opposite sex ("abstain from all appearance of evil," 1 Thess.
5:22) or anything else that would compromise the pledge
of faithfulness.

Conclusion

The person you stood with at the altar is a complex human
being. You didn't realize all that was involved in saying, "I do"
when you accepted this other person for "better or worse."
However, your mate has a right to expect that you will:

1. Understand him or her as a human being—body, soul, and
   spirit—with imperfections.
2. Accept him or her with all his or her uniqueness and differences.
3. Adapt to him or her, meeting needs and resolving conflict.
4. Appreciate him or her in a tangible way.

Are you having difficulty doing these things? there is hope. An old Chinese proverb says, "A journey of a thousand miles begins with one step."

Growth Exercises

1. Begin tonight by telling your spouse that he or she is special. Discuss together areas in which you feel strengthened by each other. Name specific things you both do or say to make you feel this way, and write down the list. The things you mention will help you recognize areas in which both of you contribute to developing each other as unique individuals.

   Seek to build up your spouse by showing how you need him or her. Express your love and seek, as much as possible, to be an encourager. Don't worry or penalize each other when you fail. Remember, no one is perfect. Ask forgiveness and get back to encouragement.

2. Read over the following list of personality characteristics and rate yourself in terms of what you are like, then what your spouse is like: (MLM—most like me; MLS—most like spouse; E—equal).

___ Dominant (argue one's point of view)	vs.	___	Passive (let others have their way most of the time)
___ Risk taker	vs.	___	Conservative
___ Confident	vs.	___	Unsure of Self
___ Structured/organized	vs.	___	Disorganized
___ Social	vs.	___	Reserved (not comfortable with lots of people)
___ Nurturer/Affectionate and (warm)	vs.	___	Aloof
___ Accepts positive attention from others	vs.	___	Reluctant to accept attention from others
___ Give others their way	vs.	___	Take charge and demand your own way
___ Trust people	vs.	___	Suspicious of people
___ Carefree	vs.	___	Anxious
___ Speak your mind	vs.	___	Guard your tongue
___ Relaxed	vs.	___	Tense
___ Rulebound	vs.	___	Spontaneous
___ Critical	vs.	___	Praising

How many opposites between you and your mate did you identify while filling out the above list? List them. How many similarities did you identify? List them.

Ask your mate to tell you how he or she thinks each of these differences can strengthen or hurt your relationship as a couple. Use the following format.

Characteristic _____ Hurt _____ Strengthen _____
Characteristic _____ Hurt _____ Strengthen _____
Characteristic _____ Hurt _____ Strengthen _____
Characteristic _____ Hurt _____ Strengthen _____

Do you think your personality can be changed? Each answer.

If you think your personality can be changed, how would you tackle the process of change?

3. To help you expand your answers to the above questions, read and discuss Ephesians 5:18.

Read Ephesians 5:15–26. List and discuss five results of being filled with the Holy Spirit.

Read Colossians 3:12–24. See if you can find and list the same five characteristics you named above that are achieved by persons who have the Word of Christ dwelling richly in their minds.

Now read James 1:5.

Next, pray and ask God to give you wisdom concerning the relationship between God's Word and God's Spirit.

Finally, discuss what you think the Bible teaches about how you could be filled with the Holy Spirit. What are your conclusions?

Do you think the negative characteristics that are part of your personality could be changed through the power of God's Holy Spirit? Do you believe that the Word of Christ must dwell richly in your individual minds before that power can become a reality in your lives? What will you need to do as a couple and as individuals to make God's Word in your minds a reality?

Additional Reading

F. Delitzsch. *A System of Biblical Psychology.* Grand Rapids: Baker, 1977.

William T. Kirwan. *Biblical Concepts for Christian Counseling.* Grand Rapids: Baker, 1984.

J. I. Packer. *Knowing Man.* Westchester, Ill.: Good News, 1978.

8

Commitment to the Control and Enjoyment of Sexuality

Carol wept uncontrollably as she told her story. She had been raised by Christian parents in a small southern town. She attended the university in her state where she was an honor student and a cheerleader. While there she met Tom. They were married after graduation. He got an excellent job. They had two children. From all appearances life could not have been more wonderful.

However, one serious problem plagued their marriage. Tom had never been faithful to Carol. It was general knowledge in the town where they lived that Tom liked women, lots of women. Carol struggled with their problem but maintained the role of the dutiful wife. Then she started having "female problems." Over a period of ten years she was infected with one sexually transmitted disease after another. Finally, she lost most of her reproductive organs to surgery. Then came the final blow. She was carrying the AIDS virus. Carol struggled with a deep anger and bitterness against Tom.

God has given people their sexual nature as part of his creative work, which he labeled good. Good sex is the will of God for every married couple. To develop intimacy, partners must maintain a commitment to a positive sexual experience. What happens in the sexual relationship is a barometer by which the couple's overall level of intimacy may be assessed. Medical doctor Ed Wheat (*Intended for Pleasure*, Revell, 1981) states, "Your sexual relationship will always mirror the larger context of your life, revealing personal fears and tensions between you and your partner, which can fluctuate, depending on how well you are getting along in other areas of your marriage. Negative feelings in a marriage will often show up first in a couple's sex life."

Sex is more than a thrilling event. Sex communicates. Sex tells persons that they are loved and welcomed to the intimate world of another. Sex speaks softly about accepting, valuing, loving, and needing. Sex generates an emotional miracle in the lives of the participants.

Intimacy is impossible without sexual fidelity. When sex leaves the boundaries of covenantal commitment, all the positive messages it sends are countered by thundering negatives. People are left hollow through sexual betrayal. Emotionally they feel little apart from anger and jealousy.

When sex is not tolerated much in a marriage, this, too, sends a message. It implies a negation of the other's value. It says, "I don't really want to share myself with you." Many Christian marriages are plagued by negative communication of this type in the sexual area. The general thought seems to be that "we are all right in the other areas; we just don't have great sex." Tragically, spouses in such a marriage deny that a sporadic sexual relationship is a negative force capable of producing great resentment in their relationship.

Sex and Sexuality

Terms are important when we speak of human sexuality. I do not use *sexuality* and *sex* interchangeably. The term *human sexuality* refers to everything we are in our maleness and femaleness. It is a much broader term than terms meant to specifically designate the sex act itself. It is meant to convey the joy of knowing someone who is different from you, someone who complements you. We experience our sexuality every day. Sexuality sets the stage but does not necessarily imply necessity for the sex act.

Doug is a freshman at the university. He has come for counseling and shares a concern over his interest in females. He states, "I don't know if I am normal or if I am sinning. I find myself looking at girls a lot. I don't think about undressing them or going to bed with them. I just admire them. I like their architecture. I like their softness and the way they talk. They see things differently than we guys do."

Doug is experiencing himself as a sexual being. His fear indicates that he hasn't had much opportunity to explore his sexual feelings with other adults. He needs to monitor his sexual interest and maintain a balance between it and the spiritual, physical, intellectual, and emotional areas of his life. However, what he is experiencing is normal, even desirable.

In the original Hebrew, Adam's response to Eve was an emotional "wow." Men and women have felt that "wow" in one another's presence since that time. That is the way God made them, and it is good.

The "wow" may lead to the point of desire. Sex is an appetite to be distinguished from sexuality. The "wow" of sexuality, when allowed to focus on another, will soon be followed by the desire for the sex act.

When God created humanity, he placed in people appetites that would ensure their personal preservation and the preservation of the human family. They do not choose to want to eat or drink. These appetites are a natural part of the life cycle and they demand attention. But people can live without sex. However, the extension of the human family makes sex necessary. God did not leave the fulfillment of the mandate to replenish the earth to chance. He placed in his creation a strong appetite that would ensure the fulfillment of the mandate. All of the appetites are connected with divine purpose and are therefore good.

Occasionally someone says, "Sex should be done away with. The world would be a better place without it." They misunderstand the Scriptures and the importance of sexuality and sex in the divine program. The real issue with sexuality and sex is not extinction but control.

In the Book of Proverbs, Solomon gives explicit directions on how God's covenantal people are to deal with appetites. He says, "When thou sittest to eat with a ruler, consider diligently what is before thee: and put a knife to thy throat, if thou be a man given to appetite. Be not desirous of his dainties: for they are deceitful meat" (Prov. 23:1–3).

The passage speaks to the issue of appetites. Solomon's concern is that people not give themselves over to appetites. The issue here is eating, but he could be talking about any appetite. When appetites are hooked to unbridled desire they go out of control.

The appetite is given a human characteristic in the text. It is deceitful. It misrepresents the truth. It says, "Feed me and I won't make you sick or fat. You won't have any negative consequences attached to satisfying me."

Diligence is required if people are to escape such deceitful propositioning. Diligence must be joined to a decision. The decision and the diligence must precede the participation. Solomon does not say to fast forever and that will take care of the appetite of hunger. Rather, he admonishes people to recognize the power and deceit of appetite and combine careful diligence, decision making, and radical restructuring of their environment so that they control the appetite.

The Song of Solomon speaks in poetic form to the issues of sexuality and sex. The poem is an exposition of the joy of marital love. A broad expanse of time is covered in the poem. It follows a young lady from prepubescence to adulthood. "We have a little sister, and she hath no breasts: what shall we do for our sister in the day when she shall be spoken for? If she be a wall, we will build upon her a palace of silver: and if she be a door, we will inclose her with boards of cedar. I am a wall, and my breasts like towers: then was I in his eyes as one that found favor" (Song of Sol. 8:8–10).

The poem is a celebration of sex and sexuality with virtue. A young girl moves from youth to womanhood. On her journey two possible options are open to her where her sexuality is concerned: She may be a door or she may be a wall. If she is a wall, her brothers propose to honor her with a palace of silver. If she is a door, they intend to lock her up in a cage fashioned from boards of cedar.

Obviously, the figure of the wall is meant to designate a position of honor with reference to her sexual experience, while the door represents a position of dishonor. As a mature woman, she announces for all to hear, "I am a wall." She is proud of her virginity and of the careful practice of virtue over all those years that made that announcement possible. How did she do it?

One verse is repeated three times in the Song of Solomon. Verse 7 in chapter 2 is repeated in chapter 3 verse 5, and in chapter 8 verse 4. It reads: "I charge you, O ye daughters of Jerusalem, by the roes, and by the hinds of the field, that ye stir not up, nor awake my love, till he please." The word *my* is in italics in the text. It has been supplied by the translators. In this case they should not have supplied the word, because they distorted the meaning of the text. She is actually saying, "I don't want you awakening my love (sexual appetite) before it is the right time." She practiced a careful and diligent control over her sexual desires. That is how she got to be a wall.

This young woman understood the importance of control and commitment. She states in chapter 8 verses 6 and 7: "Set me as a seal upon thine heart, as a seal upon thine arm: for love is strong as death; jealousy is cruel as the grave: the coals thereof are coals of fire, which hath a most vehement flame. Many waters cannot quench love, neither can the floods drown it: if a man would give all the substance of his house for love, it would utterly be contemned."

Sex is meant to be only for those who are inside the clearly defined boundaries of covenantal commitment. Sex is for marriage alone. Secularized youth will laugh at such a principle, but visit them again in their forties. They will be hollow mannequins, cheap imitations of what they might have been if only they had played by God's rules. They will not hear of control. This is the sexually-transmitted-diseases-and-abortion generation. People who played fast and loose with sex are now reaping a tragic harvest.

The young must be taught control by an older generation who model what they teach. Promiscuity is not our only dilemma.

Pornography is eating alive a generation of American males. Tom, a seminary graduate, said, "I've struggled with pornography since I was ten. I don't know whether or not I should go into the ministry. I'm afraid of being just another castaway."

Some professional counselors have normalized masturbation and not warned strongly enough of its dangers. Masturbation deceives its practitioners with increasingly subtle fantasies. Peter said, "I can't make love to my wife without a porn magazine by the bed to get me stimulated." Professionals who give young people unqualified permission to masturbate should feel an overwhelming burden to warn them of the dangers of autoerotic sex. Autoeroticism is terrifyingly addictive.

The experience of sex as a totally internalized phenomenon is at the heart of autoeroticism. Masturbation and other autoerotic forms are a journey into the self. The person closes in on himself or herself and uses the objects of such fantasy to heighten his or her sexual satisfaction. Another person merely becomes a masturbatory tool to satisfy their autoerotic urges. Such persons treat others as objects, never as persons, and rob them of their dignity and specialness. America is sexually sick because of its tolerance for tools that fuel autoeroticism. We have not yet understood that sexual addiction is every bit as imprisoning as addiction to alcohol, drugs, or food. Underrating the power of sexual addiction to enslave, we have consistently undertreated sexual addicts.

Christian Attitudes Toward Sex

As a Christian counselor I have listened to countless believers as they talked about sex. Their attitudes and questions have served to illustrate the truth that many Christians are on the right track. However, many others are hurting deeply in this important area of their lives.

Some Christians believe sex should be enjoyed. In the past decade Christians have received some valuable assistance in building biblical attitudes on the subject of sex. The recovery of the Bible as the primary counseling tool for Christian counselors has done wonders for their clients' attitudes on sex. Writers such as Jay Adams, Tim LaHaye, Ed Wheat, and the Penners deserve a major portion of the credit for these valuable changes in attitudes. They have based their approaches on Scripture but have accompanied the Scriptures with sexual information that has spelled the discovery of sexual joy for many couples.

Still we witness sexual casualties in our counseling offices. People manifest a variety of negative attitudes and hurts that we must seek to treat. Some counselors are confused. They don't know what to do with sexual feelings and sensations. Biblical teaching on sex as appetite and the emphasis on control versus elimination may prove helpful to these persons.

Some people are ignorant. They have never received even the most elementary sexual information. I remember the doctor's son who was in junior high. I was teaching a sex education course in Sunday school and had just asked if they knew where babies came from. He quickly replied, "They come out of a woman's leg." He needed reliable information from godly and concerned sources. I found out later that he got his information from his peers. Unfortunately, this is where most sexual information comes from.

Some are embarrassed. I remember when Dr. Ed Wheat conducted a seminar at our church. He began by cautioning that his material would be quite explicit and that if some would find that embarrassing they should leave. He was very gracious, and not many left initially. However, as he proceeded with his talk, several people did get up and leave. They were embarrassed. They could not deal with an honest and explicit lecture on sex. I wonder how they ever planned to give this type of information to their children. They likely could not. One of the unfortunate results of these "absent conversations" with adolescents is the alarming increase in the number of teen pregnancies.

Women who are embarrassed about sex present a unique problem to today's male. Males who are to be delivered from pornography or just deal realistically with their sight orientation to sex need wives who are comfortable with their sexuality. A man's wife should be the focus for his sensate fantasies on sexuality. If that is to be a reality he must see her and imprint her anatomy on his mind. The need for such a focus is fully developed in the Song of Solomon.

Some believe sex should be shelved and avoided. John was a new Christian. He was hesitant to talk about what was bothering him. Finally, he said, "Does being a Christian mean that you give up sex in your marriage? Before Mary and I became Christians we had a great sexual relationship. Within a matter of weeks after we were baptized and joined the church, Mary began to make excuses for not having sex. I have finally just stopped asking. Is that normal?"

I was happy to inform him that what was occurring in his marriage was not supported by Scripture. I was also careful to caution him that there might be some explanations for Mary's behavior that would cause her sexual attitudes to make sense to her. I thought it also might make sense to us as well, if we could get her to share her reasoning with us.

Mary agreed to see me, and we eventually got around to talking about Todd's concerns over the lack of sexual sharing in their marriage. She explained that prior to her marriage and conversion she had been highly promiscuous. She developed a particularly active fantasy life that reinforced her sexual involvement.

Now that Mary had become a Christian she felt guilty over her past. She felt a great sense of guilt over the fantasies that attended her sexual feelings. Mary said, "I came up with the only solution to the problem I could think of. I stopped having sex! Now I don't have the thoughts and I'm not sinning. I no longer feel guilty all the time." Mary's solution for the problem made perfect sense to her. The problem was that it didn't make sense to Todd. It couldn't. She had never discussed her problem or her solution with him.

Mary didn't understand God's purpose for sex. She didn't understand how to deal with guilt. She didn't understand the nature of biblical forgiveness, and she didn't know how to renew her mind (1 John 1:9; Ps. 32:5). She didn't understand that she had replaced one set of sinful behaviors for another. She was now defrauding her husband. After we dealt with these issues, she was able to discover a spiritual process designed by God to provide her with a new way of experiencing her sexuality, which made both her and Todd very happy.

Some believe sex is a duty. Occasionally, I have a client who believes that any personal enjoyment derived from sex is sin, but they would never consider not being available for their mate. Pam said, "I really don't care for sex but I have never denied Walter."

The male psyche is a complex entity. A man has a hard time having sex when he is always the initiator. Walter said, "I would rather go without sex than always be the one asking for it. I get the feeling that it's just for me. It makes me feel selfish. I feel like she just wants me to do my business and then leave her alone. I want a relationship with a caring-sharing partner, not just a place to do it." Pam was destroying intimacy with her attitudes about sex. When she really saw what she was doing to Walter, how much she was hurting him, and how unscriptural her attitudes were, she repented of her sin, and their relationship was transformed.

Some believe sex is to be feared. An amazingly large number of Christian marriages are not consummated within two months after the wedding. One frequent reason for this is the wife's fear of sexual intercourse. Frequently, she believes intercourse will be the source of physical pain. Sometimes she is overwhelmed by the emotional pain associated with thoughts of sexual intercourse. Sometimes males fear damage to their sexual organs.

Persons with such fears have frequently been sexually abused as children. The experience was often physically painful and usually precipitated severe-to-moderate emotional distress. As a faculty member at a Christian university I have had to face one undeniable fact: The number of male and female children being sexually abused by professing Christian dads, pastors, uncles, stepfathers, and so on is beyond belief. It is a national disgrace that parallels the national fascination with the lewd and pornographic. Medical intervention, sensitive personal counseling, and counseling of the couple can bring the couple to a point of sexual fulfillment in their marriage.

Conclusion

Sex is a wonderful gift from God to his creatures. God is not against sex but has given firm directives governing the proper use of the gift. Christians need to know the directives, how to apply them to their relationships, and how to deal with the guilt of failure through confession, forgiveness, and the practice of right sexual behaviors. Believers under control and within the context of covenantal commitment are free to experience the joy of sex.

Growth Exercises

Perfect joy and liberty in the sexual area of your lives demands that you know what the Bible says and determine with all of your hearts to program your minds and bodies for obedience.

Look up the following passages. Read each one prayerfully, say whether you agree or disagree with the principle that I think God wants us to understand from the passage, and tell each other your thoughts about it.

Twelve Biblical Principles for Heightening Sexual Intimacy

Genesis 2:24–25.

Principle One: God made man and woman sexual beings and pronounced his entire creation good. It would be a mistake to think that sex or sexual feelings were bad.

Song of Solomon 2:7; Proverbs 5:1–23; Proverbs 23:1–8.

Principle Two: It is not God's will that you somehow consign the sexual dimensions of your personhood to extinction. As with other appetites you must assume personal responsibility for control. Control, not extinction, is his plan.

Song of Solomon 8:6.

Principle Three: The only legitimate satisfaction of the sexual appetite is within covenantal commitment. This covenantal commitment is marriage and derives its legitimacy from its pledge to honor social and spiritual sanctions.

Hebrews 13:4.

Principle Four: Sex within the covenantal context and under control is not just good, it is holy.

Romans 1:21–28.

Principle Five: Some sex relationships represent a form of idolatry fashioned in the midst of personal fear and rebellion.

Proverbs 5:18, 19.

Principle Six: The sexual appetite was not just placed in humans to assure procreation. It was God's intent that it also be the source of intense pleasure for his children.

Genesis 4:1.

Principle Seven: Sexual intercourse is more than a physical act. It is a very special kind of knowing that implies deep communion, sharing, and total self-giving.

Song of Solomon 4:12; 1 Thessalonians 4:1–7; Proverbs 5:15–23; Ecclesiastes 6:9; 1 Peter 1:13–16.

Principle Eight: Sex, because of its intense nature, cannot bring ultimate joy to the participants without a complete commitment from both partners to the exclusiveness that monogamy guarantees. The absence of fidelity to one partner till death parts is a violation of divine law and produces internal rage in the person being victimized by the infidelity. Even sexual fantasy divorced from the covenantal mate can diminish the joy of sex derived from monogamous coupling.

1 Corinthians 7:1–5.

Principle Nine: Sexual intercourse is a part of the marital relationship that is absolutely necessary for the production of genuine and full unity in marriage. Only in cases where it is made impossible by other compelling reasons should its absence from marriage relationships be viewed as acceptable. In these cases both partners should understand the reasons for its absence or for their willing consent to its absence.

1 Corinthians 7:1–5.

Principle Ten: Sex should be viewed not only as a way of getting one's needs met but primarily as a way of serving one's mate. Refusal to meet a mate's sexual needs in a wholesome and healthy manner is a sin.

1 Corinthians 7:1–5.

Principle Eleven: Sex is a reciprocal right based on the reality that your body belongs to your mate. This scriptural teaching is not intended to be a license for spouse abuse but rather to emphasize the joy that spouses derive from serving one another in a satisfying and healthy sexual manner. In such a setting sex is personal and holy, a complex meeting of both mates' feelings, thoughts, and sensations.

Genesis 2:18–25.

Principle Twelve: Sex is fully satisfying only when two persons possessed of expanding individual identities come to the experience. Each one comes prepared to give and demand. Each one remains intermittently independent and dependent. Both fill the void in the other and discover in the filling a developing fullness in themselves.

Additional Reading

Clifford and Joyce Penner. *The Gift of Sex.* Waco: Word, 1981.
John White. *Eros Defiled.* Downers Grove: InterVarsity, 1977.
Earl P. Wilson. *Sexual Sanity.* Downers Grove: InterVarsity, 1977.

9

Commitment to Communication

When Peg and I got married we understood the meaning of commitment. My mother had stayed with my father through years of alcoholism. She modeled commitment. Peg's mother and father had modeled commitment through their good and bad times, also. We had a rich heritage in the area of commitment. We, too, were committed for life when we walked away from the altar in that small church.

We had no idea that the greatest challenge to our commitment would come from our own faltering skills in communication. But we would learn about that soon enough. As I look back, it's amazing that the preacher never mentioned the word *communication* to us in the one premarital session we had.

I remember thinking only once about what communication would be like. I wondered what we could possibly talk about for the rest of our lives. How could we possibly have something new to talk about every morning? Over the years that fear vanished. We soon discovered that having something to talk about would not be a problem. However, communication in a constructive rather than destructive manner would represent a major challenge. We discovered some roadblocks to communication as well as some communication facilitators.

Roadblocks to Communication

Communication is the key to the development of any growing relationship. Poor communication between couples is the number one reason for marital failure. Nothing they can do holds more potential for enriching intimacy in marriage than taking the time to learn how to communicate in an effective and encouraging manner with their mates.

Sally and Jim had come to talk about their marriage. She felt depressed over their relationship. Jim believed that he was an excellent communicator, but Sally felt their communication was poor. As we began the first session I heard and saw the reason for Sally's concern over the issue of communication.

Jim was very good at expressing his thoughts. However, he adopted a tone and body position that conveyed an air of total superiority. He suggested at one point that "we all know how women are." He seemed to delight in ordering Sally to listen to him. He often used extreme words like *always* and *never.* He felt good when he could correct what he perceived to be mistakes in her thought or reporting. Communication seemed to be a power game with him. He frequently advised and criticized Sally. He did not talk with Sally; he lectured her. He never looked in her eyes while he talked, and he appeared to listen to her only for the purpose of destroying her presentations. He constantly used an "accusatory you" as he addressed problems instead of the "collective we." When she attempted to defend herself, he would get a little smile around his mouth, slump back into the chair, and lapse into silence or patronize her with "Maybe someday you'll understand."

His every word and movement suggested that he had no respect for Sally. He was frequently sarcastic and took delight in shifting the blame to her for most of the problems in the marriage. When she tried to respond, he acted like a defense attorney and attempted to destroy her with cross examination. No wonder she was depressed. When he didn't seem to be able to win with his argument he would move to a more threatening expression like, "Well, I'm soon gone anyway."

We generally think of communication as just speaking. In fact, much of our communication is nonverbal. We communicate by what we do not say. At one point in my session with Sally and Jim she stated, "I don't think he loves me anymore." I watched Jim to see how he would respond to this need in Sally's life. He said nothing. He deliberately intended to deepen her hurt by withholding from her what she clearly had expressed a need for. The silent treatment or the ignoring of a request for encouragement can do great damage to communication.

This exchange between Sally and Jim illustrates a negative communication style that can destroy intimacy. I see this kind of insensitivity demonstrated all the time. People who are victims of it show all the signs of fatigue that we would expect to see in a soldier returning from a heavy combat area. James was certainly correct when he stated: "Even so the tongue is a little member, and boasteth great things. Behold how great a matter a little fire kindleth" (James 3:5)!

God Is a Communicator

The Bible places high value on good communication. The Creator is a communicator. He consistently accepts the responsibility for initiating communication. Prior to human sin he spoke with the man and woman and blessed them with his speech and presence. Genesis 1:28 says: "And God blessed them, and God said unto them, Be fruitful, and multiply, and replenish the earth, and subdue it: and have dominion over the fish of the sea, and over the fowl of the air, and over every living thing that moveth upon the earth."

God's desire for communication transcends the sin of his creatures. He did not abandon his pursuit of communication just because of the entry of sin into the lives of his creatures. In Genesis 3:8–10 we read: "And they heard the voice of the LORD God walking in the garden in the cool of the day: and Adam and his wife hid themselves from the presence of the LORD God amongst the trees of the garden. And the LORD God called unto Adam, and said unto him, Where art thou? And he said, I heard thy voice in the garden, and I was afraid, because I was naked; and I hid myself."

God pursues those whom he loves and seeks to communicate with them. Sin, on the other hand, produces in the life of the creature a desire to disengage from the communication process, to go and hide. To those who would hide, God says, "Come now, and let us reason together, . . . though your sins be as scarlet, they shall be as white as snow; though they be red like crimson, they shall be as wool" (Isa. 1:18).

God provides those who will hear his words with a covering for their sin that allows them to be reconciled to himself. Genesis 3:21 reads: "Unto Adam also and to his wife did the Lord God make coats of skins, and clothed them." This has always been the Creator's response. When those whom he loves are confused and disengaged from the communication process, he provides them with that which is necessary to effect reconciliation. His love will not allow him to stand over against them without first seeking their restoration. Hosea captures this unfathomable love of God when he says: "How shall I give thee up, Ephraim? how shall I deliver thee, Israel? how shall I make thee as Admah? how shall I set thee as Zeboim? mine heart is turned within me, my repentings are kindled together. I will not execute the fierceness of my anger" (Hos. 11:8, 9).

Ultimately, this love would culminate in the coming of God in human flesh. John beautifully captures that coming when he says: "For God so loved the world, that he gave his only begotten Son, that whosoever believeth in him should not perish, but have everlasting life. For God sent not his Son into the world to condemn the world: but that the world through him might be saved" (John 3:16–17).

God entered human history to personally become the covering for humanity's sin. John again captures this truth when he says: "My little children, these things write I unto you, that ye sin not. And if any man sin, we have an advocate with the Father, Jesus Christ the righteous: and he is the propitiation for our sins: and not for ours only, but also for the sins of the whole world" (1 John 2:1–2). In the New Testament the Creator is doing just what he did in the Old Testament. He is covering the sin of his creatures.

His motive is a love that defies human description. His method is consistent. "Without shedding of blood there is no remission" (Heb. 9:22). His mission is the same throughout human history. Paul captures this mission when he states: "To wit, that God was in Christ, reconciling the world unto himself, not imputing their trespasses unto them; and hath committed unto us the word of reconciliation (2 Cor. 5:19).

The entire Bible is about communication. God desires to communicate with his creatures. He created them to communicate with him. When that communication is interrupted by rebellion and sin he immediately sets in motion a process to restore the broken communication. He loves so deeply that he is willing to become the bridge across the broken expanse between humanity and himself. The bridge is formed from his own body and sacrifice.

The bridge opens up the possibility of fellowship with the Creator. John captures this beautiful truth when he says: "Our fellowship is with the Father, and with his Son Jesus Christ. And these things write we unto you, that your joy may be full" (1 John 1:3–4).

John further states that the God of communication purposes that "ye also may have fellowship with us" (1 John 1:3). A friend recently wrote and closed his letter with these words: "Yours because his." Therein lies the secret for marital communication. People who are his seek to imitate his heart (Eph. 5:1–2). They are absolutely determined to communicate with their mates because God is absolutely determined to communicate with them. The choice to communicate is not based on personal gain or pleasure. It is rooted in the conviction that we are called to implement in our relationships the same concern for ongoing communication that grips the heart of God.

No wonder Paul says that poor habits of communication grieve God the Holy Spirit. He says: "Let no corrupt communication proceed out of your mouth, but that which is good to the use of edifying, that it may minister grace unto the hearers. And grieve not the Holy Spirit of God" (Eph. 4:29, 30). The absence of kindness, tenderheartedness, and forgiveness in the speech and conduct of God's children is a cause of grievous injury to God. They stand in the world as God's ambassadors (2 Cor. 5:20). When they speak they speak for God. This is not just true of what they say in the pulpit or the marketplace. It is a matter of the gravest importance to recognize the truth of Christians' ambassadorship as they speak to their wives, husbands, children, and friends. When they as God's ambassadors wound one another through cutting speech, they grieve God. Tragically, that may not be a cause of great upset to some who claim to know Christ. However, for a genuine believer the thought of grieving God is cause for deep remorse. Only one thing can cure such acts of barbarism: repentance.

Repentance and Communication

The components of healthy communication can be observed in God's communication with his creatures. Love, patience, gentleness, goodness, faith, meekness, forgiveness, exhortation, encouragement, and a host of other relationship-enhancing characteristics are evidenced in God's communication. What are partners to do when these traits are not characteristic of the communication patterns with their mates? Frequently they approach their problems in communication with an arsenal of rules on communication. Although these sometimes prove helpful, they are often like putting a Band-Aid on a bullet wound. One or both parties really need their attitudes overhauled. New skills in the mind will not accomplish this. A change of mind and heart is required.

Paul had some communication problems with the Corinthian believers. He wrote of his attempts to resolve these problems: "O ye Corinthians, our mouth is open unto you, our heart is enlarged. Ye are not straitened in us but ye are straitened in your own bowels" (2 Cor. 6:11–12). There was a blockage in the lines of affection between Paul and the Corinthian believers. Something prohibited Paul and those believers from enjoying fellowship with one another. A communication breakdown had occurred. Paul did several things to make reconciliation possible.

First, he clarified responsibilities. When a communication breakdown occurs, all parties must be willing to examine themselves. Each must look for any contribution they may have made to the breakdown. Paul indicated that he had participated in such a process of examination and asked the Corinthian believers to do the same.

Second, he courageously and compassionately identified the precise area where the problem lay. He was willing to be the problem, but in this case the problem was with the Corinthian believers. The constriction of emotions that was causing the communication breakdown was in the minds and hearts of the Corinthians. Paul was certain of that.

Third, Paul let them know that he was 100 percent committed to reconciliation. He asked them to receive him (2 Cor. 7:2). He let them know that he was always open for the discussion of reconciliation. His heart was enlarged, filled with love for those believers. The shortage of emotional energy required for reconciliation was in their lives, not in Paul's.

Fourth, Paul exhorted them through his recommendation of a cure that was of sufficient strength to smash down the walls between them. Paul wanted Christian love to flow between them again. They were his children, and he prayed for the enlargement of their hearts (2 Cor. 6:13). This enlargement would only occur if they participated in an act of repentance.

Paul did not believe that teaching new communication skills would resolve his problem with the Corinthian believers. He believed that only the spiritual power released through repentance would open the broken lines of communication between them.

Suppose you started to experience chest pains and went to the doctor. The doctor told you that the arteries carrying blood to your heart were closing down. The life of your heart muscle is a serious issue. What if he recommended decreasing the amount of sugar in your daily coffee as the treatment of choice? I think you would look for another doctor. Those arteries would have to be opened; blood must reach the heart muscle to ensure its life. Technology is available to accomplish this, and we thank God for it. The administration of that technology is not without pain and discomfort, but it is often highly effective.

Paul told the Corinthian believers that the treatment of choice for their "heart condition" was not without pain. He had mixed feelings over bringing them into an experience of sorrow. However, he believed in the absolute necessity of what he had done. He brought them to a point of reality regarding their sin and called them to godly sorrow over their wrong beliefs which had produced the communication breakdown.

The Corinthians listened to Paul and received the ministry of the Holy Spirit. They repented. This was a miracle. They were willing to accept responsibility for and correct their sinful actions, identify and correct their sinful thoughts, and use the energy generated from repentance to open the lines of communication between Paul and themselves. No wonder Paul was rejoicing (2 Cor. 7:9). He was witnessing the transformation of believers that is made possible through the miracle of repentance.

Repentance is in short supply in today's marriages. One reason for its scarcity lies in the fact that counselors and preachers don't teach and preach the necessity for it. Frequently my clients need not only to learn how to communicate more effectively; they also need to repent. Certain characteristics are present in the lives of those who have repented (2 Cor. 7:11). A carefulness characterizes their speech and conduct. They are deeply concerned about walking before God and others with a conscience that is clear of any known offense. They get angry with their own sins and the sins of others. They have new respect and fear for the power of sin to deceive and ruin people's lives. They have a deep desire for the Word of God, for fellowship with the Spirit of God, and for fellowship with other believers. They manifest a zeal for the work of God. They believe in fasting and keeping their bodies and minds under the domination of God's truth and Spirit. They don't mind proving their sincerity. They believe what Paul wrote: "But let every man prove his own work, and then shall he have rejoicing in himself alone, and not in another" (Gal. 6:4).

Repentance needs to be mutual if it is to exercise its full power to generate marital intimacy. Paul and the Corinthians both needed to go through the examination process and stand ready to repent over identified sin. Marriages in which lasting intimacy is a reality are made up of husbands and wives who are always open to repentance when they identify the need for dealing with sin.

Forgiveness, which is also essential for ongoing intimacy, should not be given without clear evidence of repentance. Too often weak mates stand ready to forgive unrepentant mates. Jesus said, "Take heed to yourselves: If thy brother trespass against thee rebuke him, and if he repent, forgive him" (Luke 17:3). Forgiveness that is cheap (devoid of repentance in the sinner) is granted by persons who lack a biblical sense of personal worth and mission. Intimacy is impossible for such persons.

Believers have the responsibility to examine one another and provoke one another unto love and good works (Heb. 10:24). This responsibility should be taken seriously by mates. No one is in a position to take another person to greater heights of spiritual achievement then that person's mate. Each one's feelings over the interchange will vary from enthusiasm to resentment, but the process must go on. Communication between mates will break down without reciprocal repentance. An attitude of love and mutual repentance over discovered sin will enable a couple to achieve levels of marital intimacy they never dreamed possible.

The Holy Spirit and Communication

I don't think it is an accident that one of the greatest passages on communication in Scripture occurs in the same area as a discussion of the filling of the Holy Spirit. All the characteristics Christians need for communication are the result of the Holy Spirit's ministry in their lives. His power produces repentance. They will themselves to be channels through which the energy of repentance may reach into the world of relationships, but the provisioned power is his. His fruit heals relationships. Consider this list of relationship enhancers: love, joy, peace, gentleness, goodness, faith, meekness, self-control. These allies of restoration and healing are not ours, they are his.

I desperately need the Holy Spirit in his fullness. I need his fruit to be my daily offering to those around me. I believe this will happen only if my mind is filled richly with God's Word. The correspondence between the characteristics of God's servants found in Ephesians 5:18–33 and Colossians 3:12–25 is striking. In Ephesians 5 the characteristics are derived through the filling of the Spirit, while in Colossians 3 they are derived through the Word of God dwelling richly in the mind of the believer. The Word and the Spirit are both required to achieve the fruit that provides energy for the building of intimacy. Strong, fruitful individuals committed to him will be committed to each other. What passes between them will be his fruit, and it will fuel intimacy, not destroy it.

We had begun to cut wood for the upcoming winter cold. I bought a new axe handle from the hardware store, because the old one was getting chewed up. I placed it in a high place in the basement and planned to fit it to the axe head later on.

One evening I had a few spare moments so I went to get the axe handle. To my surprise, when I picked it up I found someone had been working on it already. For a moment I was dumbfounded. I let out one of those fatherly cries, "Who ruined this axe handle?"

My son's eyes immediately filled with tears. "I did!" he replied.

I wanted to lecture him, but the Holy Spirit wouldn't let me. An inner prompting took over. I am grateful for that inner prompting, for I saw my son's heart. He had only wanted to help, and I loved him for it. I said, "You know what? The first time I tried to fit one of these things to the axe head I butchered it, too. Let's go get another handle, and this time we will fit it to the head together."

I call this experience my "theology of the axe handle." I had been reading my Bible and depending upon God's Spirit for wisdom each day. In this critical moment the Holy Spirit flooded over my turbulence and gave me a self-control that resulted in a healing dialog between my son and me. The Holy Spirit brought order out of chaos, understanding out of confusion, and self-control out of turbulence. Where the Holy Spirit dwells in fullness, intimacy abounds.

Conclusion

Nothing is more important for you as a couple than learning to communicate with each other. How is it going, wife? husband?

People don't learn how to be good communicators overnight. The more you read the Word, listen to the Holy Spirit, and deal repentantly with sins of omission and commission the better you get at the process that is the lifeblood of marital and family relationships. The following growth exercise is designed to be done over a long period of time. It contains many small skills that you need to pray about and then apply to your communication opportunities with people. I have set it up so you can keep a record of your progress by providing you with a place to record the date you tried to apply the instruction and a space for recording the results. I suggest that you read the growth exercise over in one sitting and then prayerfully work on the different skills one or a few at a time. God bless you as you seek to follow the model of our heavenly Father and become a good communicator.

Growth Exercises

I introduced you to Jim and Sally at the beginning of this chapter. Jim's initial need was for repentance of his sin against God and his wife. Once that repentance was an accomplished fact he needed a lot of specific instructions on how to deal with some very bad communication patterns he had developed over the years. The following material on communication can be helpful to you after the issues of repentance and reliance on the Holy Spirit have been adequately addressed.

Think of communication for reconciliation as a process that has three phases: the initiation phase, the continuation phase, and the termination phase. Each of these phases is important for the development of intimacy. Following are some principles that can help to assure successful communication in each phase. Because you undoubtedly are going to get a chance to use each of these principles at some point, you will be able to record your application of them.

The Initiation Phase

You need to build a bridge between the two of you. The intent is to join your mate through communication supported by love. You must convince the other person that you are completely committed to reconciliation. You are not out to score points; you just want to get back on track for the relationship and for the Lord. This is where people often fall short. Sometimes in my marriage I know the water has been stirred and I'm in trouble. I find that I often get more interested in justifying my viewpoint during these times than in seeking understanding. Several things should be prominent during this phase of the communication process if understanding rather than turmoil is to increase between you.

Express commitment: You might say this: "I want to let you know as we begin this conversation how much I love you (1 Cor. 13:4–8). I want you to know that I am 100 percent committed to you and the building of our relationship (2 Cor. 6:11, 12; 7:3; 2 Tim. 1:3–5). Nothing can change my love for you, and even though there are problems right now, I know with God's help we can overcome them."

Date I tried it: _____
How it went: _____

Model humility: You might say this: "I could be totally wrong in the way I feel about this situation, but I need to check with you to see if my perceptions are right or wrong" (Gal. 6:1; 1 Tim. 1:15).

Date I tried it: _____
How it went: _____

Speak with hopeful optimism: You might say this: "I know we can work this problem out. I am convinced that the preservation of this relationship is worth whatever price we have to pay (Rom. 15:1–7). Even though at times it seems our problems are hard to solve, I know that nothing is too hard for the LORD" (Gen. 18:14).

Date I tried it: _____
How it went: _____

The Continuation Phase

The focus here is on maintaining a positive tone that will allow communication to continue to the point of resolution and reconciliation. Several elements related to communication should be carefully considered. You need to give careful attention to maintaining a positive attitude during this phase. In the Song of Solomon we find an excellent example of how to establish and maintain a positive cycle of communication. Solomon, recording the conversation between the lovers, says: "I am the rose of Sharon, and the lily of the valleys. As the lily among the thorns, so is my love among the daughters. As the apple tree among the trees of the woods, so is my beloved among the sons. I sat down under his shadow with great delight and his fruit was sweet to my taste" (Song of Sol. 2:1–3). The exchange between these lovers is very positive. It is a discussion that leads its participants into a deepening experience of intimacy.

She begins the discussion with a statement of self-depreciation. She describes herself as a rose of Sharon and lily of the valley (ordinary flowers that grew wild everywhere and were of little value). He counters that she is like a lily in a field of thorns. To him she is outstanding. She possesses great beauty. She then responds and affirms his immense value to her.

This positive cycle of communication is in stark contrast to the negative cycles that many couples experience. Communication can be positive, encouraging, and continually enriching if you keep the following elements in mind.

Pay attention: Listen carefully to what your spouse is saying. (Prov. 18:13; Eph. 4:32; 1 Cor. 16:14; Titus 3:2; James 1:19).

Support the other person. Attempt to listen with good eye contact, nodding positively, and maintaining warm facial expressions.

Date I tried it: _____
How it went: _____

Be sensitive to feelings: Don't just hear the words; try to be sensitive to the feelings behind the words. Don't analyze everything. Listen some with your heart and just accept the other's feelings. You would be surprised how much better your ears work when you keep your mouth closed.

Date I tried it: _____
How it went: _____

Pay attention to what isn't being said: Try to notice what your spouse is not saying. The absence of certain words can be important.

Date I tried it: _____
How it went: _____

Pay attention to body language: Watch the other's body language. Does he or she appear tense or uncomfortable? Can your body language put your spouse at ease?

Date I tried it: _____
How it went: _____

Seek to understand: Ask for a clarification whenever you are not sure what is meant.

Date I tried it: _____
How it went: _____

Listen a lot: Don't talk a lot initially; just listen. Don't offer interpretations or opinions on what is said. Simply encourage your spouse to continue sharing thoughts and feelings.

Date I tried it: _____
How it went: _____

Request further information: Get all the facts before responding (James 1:19).

Date I tried it: _____
How it went: _____

Summarize to make certain you are hearing correctly: Ask for the purpose of clarification: "Is this what you think and the way you feel?" "I thought I heard you say this. . . . Is this correct?"

Date I tried it: _____
How it went: _____

Respond carefully. (Prov. 15:23, 28; 29:20). Make certain that now is the best time for this discussion (Eccl. 3:7).

Pray for wisdom: Ask God for wisdom to make effective responses (Eccl. 12:9–14; James 1:5).

Don't let your feelings get in the way: Feelings can support conversation if they are not based on reaction. Don't get angry and quarrel. If you are getting angry, call a time out; leave and come back later. Remember, this conversation is to help the other person and your relationship, not for you to get something off your chest (Prov. 15:1; 25:15; 1 Peter 2:23).

Think carefully about what you are going to say: Make certain your brain is fully in gear before you put your mouth in motion. Choose your words carefully (Prov. 18:15; Phil. 3:15–16).

Date I tried it: _____
How it went: _____

Keep hope alive throughout the process: Express confidence in your relationship and in God's power to get you both on track again. Focus on the strength of your partner and your strength as a team (2 Tim. 1, 2; Acts 15:36–40; 2 Tim. 4:11).

Date I tried it: _____
How it went: _____

Identify specific goals: Ask God to help you focus on goals to work on that will serve to enhance your relationship. Promise to do your best to accomplish the goals (Phil. 4:5–9).

Date I tried it: _____

How it went: _____

Get outside help: When you are not sure what to do or say, get help from a pastor, Christian counselor, or trusted lay person (Prov. 24:6).

Date I tried it: _____

How it went: _____

The Termination Phase

The focus here is on moving prayerfully to reconciliation and resolution. If that does not happen, continue praying and seek competent assistance such as professional counsel. The following elements should be part of closing off your discussion.

Restate your commitment to the relationship (2 Cor. 7:3).

Date we did it:_____

What happened: _____

Restate your confidence in God's ability to provide the wisdom for the healing and enrichment of this relationship (2 Tim. 3:15–17).

Date we did it:_____

What happened: _____

Reaffirm your desire to be God's people. Surrender the control of your lives and resources. Commit yourselves to doing things God's way. Summarize assigned goals and pray together, asking for God's power for achievement of your reconciliation (2 Cor. 7:1–11).

Date we did it:_____

What happened: _____

Additional Reading

Lawrence Crabb, Jr. *The Marriage Builder.* Grand Rapids: Zondervan, 1982.

Roger Fish and William Ury. *Getting to Yes: Negotiating Agreement Without Giving In.* New York: Penguin, 1981).

Joyce Hugget. *Creative Conflict: How to Confront and Stay Friends.* Downers Grove: InterVarsity, 1984.

10

Commitment to Companioning

The snow was falling so hard I could scarcely see my feet. I was cold and had already walked two and a half miles. Where was I going? I was on my way to see my friend, the girl I wanted to marry. I had made the trip several times before. No adversity would keep me from getting to my goal. I loved spending time with my friend. I loved hearing the sound of her voice. I loved being myself when I was with her.

Relationships frequently start with this kind of enthusiasm and then cool. This is tragic. *The strength of a marriage is directly related to the couple's desire for togetherness.* The average Christian marriage that fails does so because of a lack of appreciation for the importance of companioning. Two persons who understand commitment grow apart because their understanding does not extend to devoting large blocks of time to the ongoing development of their friendship.

Intimacy is possible only when two persons continue to engage in activities that build their friendship. Patricia Gundry in her book *Heirs Together* (Zondervan, 1980) states, "Nowadays, couples want more from marriage in a close personal way; we long for a relationship that is intimate and loving." A mate who is a good provider or a capable housekeeper is not enough. Couples need and require from each other a strong sharing of common

123

experiences that result in the continuing enrichment of their relationship.

This quality of sharing demands that the two persons be in the same place at the same time. This seems obvious, but in the closing hours of the twentieth century the need exists to emphasize this requirement for strengthening intimacy. Mates cannot enhance their companioning if their schedules place them consistently in different geographical areas. If he is working nights and she is working days, companioning may not be impossible, but it will be difficult at best. If he is going to church meetings every night or she is off with her friends, companioning will be weakened. In short, companioning demands that the two organize their time to clearly place the building of the relationship very high on their personal agenda.

I loved being married. It was great having Peg close by to share with. I had to finish one more year at Bible school when we tied the knot. Our married life started in a twelve-by-fifteen room over the school gym (the price was right). I was still very near my school friends of the past two years, and breaking away from them was tough.

I never will forget the look on Peg's face when I came in late for supper one night. I had to learn that my allocation of time needed to be brought into line with my new commitment. She was now to be my best friend. She was to be more important than basketball and hanging around the dorm with the guys. This importance had to be processed into time invested. She had the right to expect it. Knowing my responsibility and bringing my life into conformity with its demands represented a major challenge for the next several years.

The Bible on Companioning

I frequently chafed under the demands of my new responsibilities. I soon developed a number of excuses for not always responding positively to her needs. Some of my favorite rationalizations were: Nobody's perfect; I deserve this time for myself; I've been working real hard lately; She is so unfair! She expects too much. I often found myself wrestling with my selfish responses to problems that developed in our relationship and never could feel good about those negative responses. I knew the Bible taught that Peg and I were to be companions who were enjoying, not just tolerating, our relationship.

Sometimes I felt some of the loneliness that Adam must have felt before Eve's creation. Those were the times when we were at odds and isolated from one another. God had said, "It is not good that the man should be alone" (Gen. 2:18). I knew in those times of isolation that God had been right.

I also knew that when Peg and I were properly related to him and to one another, we experienced life on a higher level. Solomon captured the agony and the ecstasy of marital relationships in writing this:

> There is one alone, and there is not a second; yea, he hath neither child nor brother: yet is there no end of all his labor; neither is his eye satisfied with riches; neither saith he, for whom do I labor; and bereave my soul of good? This is also vanity, yea, it is a sore travail. Two are better than one; because they have a good reward for their labor. For if they fall, the one will lift up his fellow: but woe to him that is alone when he falleth; for he hath not another to help him up" (Eccles. 4:8–10).

Reward is the fruit of our laboring together. We derive a special joy from accomplishing a task together. This reward spontaneously erupts when we experience the truth that together we represent a force greater than the sum of our individual strengths. The reward of our united accomplishments creates a near addiction to working at tasks together. Thus united we seldom find ourselves desiring to go it alone.

The marriage relationship with its scriptural emphasis on companioning is of great importance to God. Little wonder he said, "Therefore shall a man leave his father and his mother, and shall cleave unto his wife: and they shall be one flesh" (Gen. 2:24). Leaving, cleaving, and weaving involve more than intellectual commitment. They imply the investment of time and energy to enrich relationships.

To ensure the proper investment of time for building the relationship, God laid out specific instructions for newlyweds in the Old Testament. Moses said, "When a man hath taken a new wife, he shall not go out to war, neither shall he be charged with any business: but he shall be free at home one year, and shall cheer up his wife which he hath taken" (Deut. 24:5). God expected husbands to invest time in their wives. The responsibility for this focused investment has never been withdrawn in Scripture.

God was intensely angry with Israel. The elders in Israel inquired of God to discover the reason for his anger. God answered: "Yet ye say, Wherefore? Because the LORD hath been witness between thee and the wife of thy youth, against whom thou hast dealt treacherously: yet is she thy companion, and the wife of thy covenant" (Mal. 2:14). Men in Israel had become hard of heart. They did not see God's unique gifts in their wives. They divorced them with calloused indifference. God hated this indifference that allowed for such easy divorce.

Paul said, "Husbands, love your wives, even as Christ also loved the church, and gave himself for it" (Eph. 5:25). Love for their wives was far from ancient Israel's men and so it remains for man until the present hour. Seldom do we meet a man who seeks to love his wife with the same selflessness that Christ loves his church.

Can you imagine Jesus Christ saving us and then declining to spend any further time with us? Suppose he were to say, "I've secured heaven for you; now I must be busy with other tasks. Don't bother me with the burden of daily conversation." The Christ of Scripture would never say such a thing. He saved us to have a relationship with us (1 John 1:3–4). Fullness of joy is discovered in ongoing fellowship. Likewise, the reward to be derived from the marriage relationship is only for those who spend time cheering one another.

The Shulamite maiden knew why she was eager for the presence of her beloved. She said, "This is my beloved, and this is my friend, O daughters of Jerusalem" (Song of Sol. 5:16). The biblical picture of intimacy includes the concept of friendship. A man once said, "Don't marry someone you won't want for a friend." I thought that a strange thing to say, but over the years I have seen many people marry who had no resources with which to build a friendship. Those marriages never lasted.

Friendship is absolutely essential if marital intimacy is to be developed by a couple. Friends each possess strengths. Each brings something to give to the other. Each receives the other's gift with gratitude. Neither need ever attain perfection. The celebration of what they bring to each other is enough; it overshadows any and all inadequacies in the giver.

Companion-friends can either build or destroy their relationship. Understanding of both the negative and positive cycles of companioning can help to assure the successful building of intimacy through friendship.

A Negative Companioning Cycle

Mark had come to see me because he had just broken up with his girlfriend. After talking with him for a while I discovered this was his fourth relationship with a girl that had started well and ended abruptly. He said, "In the past two years I have been in and out of four important relationships. Something is wrong, and I don't know what it is. Why do my relationships start off so well and end up being such disasters?"

Disastrous relationships often follow a negative relationship cycle. The relationship begins with great excitement but ends because of some destructive needs that exist in one or both of the participants. The doomed cycle generally contains these elements or stages:

> Attraction Stage
> Infatuation Stage
> Cooperation Stage
> Management Stage
> Domination Stage
> Argument Stage
> Retaliation Stage
> Isolation Stage
> Termination Stage

These stages are clearly discernable in the unhappy relationships engaged in by many couples. At its inception a negative companioning cycle closely resembles a positive one. The suggestion of serious problems begins with the intensity of the infatuation phase and the quick transition to the management and domination stages.

The *attraction* stage is the "wow" stage. This represents Adam's response to Eve the first time he saw her (Gen. 2:23). The stage is characterized by an absorbing interest in some dimension of the other person's life or personality. The area of interest is most frequently the physical. The strong powers of attraction at work during this phase are primarily rooted in biological need.

In the *infatuation* stage the two persons are consumed with their relationship. The relationship has moved to the point where all energies are directed toward being with each other. There is an addictive passion for that which is desirable about the desired person. This passion takes over and quickly overwhelms any concerns over potentially negative dimensions in the relationship. Reason is seemingly dismissed, and feelings totally dominate the relationship.

Cooperation now becomes a major feature of the relationship. However, the cooperation is rooted in personal motives which are self-serving. Both persons are willing to practice self-denial and forego personal gain for the sake of being with each other. The desire to be together is often so strong that the couple exists over against all previous relationships (parents, teachers, friends). However, this self-absorption frequently results in an internal conflict for the couple over who ultimately gets first chance to have his or her needs met in the relationship.

Cooperation that is self-serving soon focuses on the *management* of the other person. Manipulative persons manage all of the resources around them, including other persons, for the specific purpose of self-enrichment. During this phase the self-centeredness of the manipulator becomes fully obvious to everyone. Cooperation is no longer possible, and the potential for intimacy is destroyed. The attraction that produced the infatuation is only a memory that no longer makes any rational sense, although it may live on in the emotions. Managed persons at some point offer resistance. They sense the impending death of their own personalities through the oppressive domination of their self-centered companions. They understand intuitively that such a death is a form of strangulation that signals the end of any potential for an intimate relationship. They resist.

Their resistance is met with an attempt at total *domination*. The domination may be physical, intellectual, or spiritual. Battering, verbal abuse, and twisted views on submission are all subtly used by manipulators to effect the goal of total domination. People go on dominating and being dominated for varying periods of time. People who are willing to say good-bye to any sense of personal identity and self-respect will sometimes stay in these abusive relationships for years. Most, however, will eventually resist this depersonalization.

The dominated frequently begin to *argue* back. Their verbal responses often serve to ignite power issues for their mates. Abusive mates can tolerate *absolutely* no challenges to their authority; they meet challenge with displays of power that serve to reinforce their domination. This may bring couples to the attention of neighbors, police, and the courts. In time it may also bring them into the counselor's office. Couples who are involved in this stage are often professing Christians. Dominance and battering are serious problems in the church today.

When no effective means of coping with domination are present, *retaliation* often becomes the course of choice. The battered person figures out a way to get even. This has been the motivation behind some well-publicized incidents of family violence. Rather than ceasing to exist as people these battered individuals strike back. Their choices are often silent tributes to the inability of the churches, police, and courts to intervene for the victims of family violence.

Energy for positive relationships is gone when couples have traveled through this degenerative relationship cycle. Energy spent, the battered individual moves into *isolation*. In the isolation stage the person struggles between the rational requirements for dealing with the abuse and the remaining emotions of love toward the abuser.

While in isolation some sense of self-respect, identity, and integrity is regained that supplies the person with the energy to rebound. The manipulative dominator tries to woo the mate back, still needing someone to feed on. The battered individual may choose to utilize the energy gained during isolation to return and work at rebuilding the relationship with the abuser.

The battered person's return is supported by emotional energy regained through separation from the abuser. The abuser often demonstrates a "miraculous" interest in cooperation. However, without extensive counseling, the needs that spawned the abuse are still firmly in place, and the negative cycle begins again.

Eventually, the abusive cycle will *terminate*. The abused person will finally feel that survival of the self is impossible with the abuser. Frequently, this termination will be hastened by the realization that the children are also being used as resources by the manipulative dominator. Sensing that intimacy is impossible when they are merely resources to be dominated, some persons have found the courage to terminate.

This negative pattern is often preventable. Degenerative patterns in relationships can be stopped when couples recognize their destructive potential and decide to initiate change. Many persons are imprisoned by selfish commitment to their *own* needs. The only answer for them is personal repentance. They need an experience with Jesus Christ that sets them free from egoism and provides them with the power to live life differently. This experience should be accompanied by counseling that focuses on the damaging relational patterns that have become habitual.

A Positive Companioning Cycle

The positive companioning cycle differs from the negative cycle in some important ways. The following stages are discernable in positive companioning:

> Attraction Stage
> Commitment Stage
> Adjustment Stage

Argument Stage
Cooperation Stage
Edification Stage

Positive companioning contains a strong dimension of *attraction*. Couples who companion well do so because there is something about their mates that they find compellingly attractive. The attraction may be rooted in mental, social, artistic, spiritual, physical, or countless other skills or attributes possessed by the other. The attraction is not based on senseless infatuation but is supported by reason. The attraction is not only reasonable to the couple but makes sense to others who love them. It does not generate a mentality in the couple that sets them in opposition to those who love them; rather, it results in a strengthening of the individuals that causes others (parents, pastors, teachers) to celebrate the couple's togetherness. All areas of each individual's personality will be enriched because of the energy supplied by this attraction. The mate enters through the doorway of attraction to bless and enrich the whole person.

Physical attraction is good. The Scriptures are very specific on the power of the physical to enhance companioning. Passages like Song of Solomon 4:1–7 and 5:10–16 leave no room to depreciate the value of physical attraction. This attraction always operates best when it is kept within the dual structures of covenant and control (Song of Sol. 2:7, 8:6). Intimacy cannot exist for couples who merely celebrate the physical. The celebration of the physical should provide an energy for building other areas of the relationship.

Attraction must culminate in exclusive *commitment* to the other individual if intimacy is to be achieved. This exclusivity is not rooted in the desire to control or isolate that person. On the contrary, it is calculated to produce a sense of safety and trust. Intimacy is impossible unless it is continuously reinforced by companioning based on a foundation of trust. Jealousy grows in the absence of trust. The tragedy of jealousy is that its power to destroy is equaled only by the destructive force of the grave (Song of Sol. 8:6). How different is the relationship where trust is the predominant theme. Solomon says, "The heart of her husband doth safely trust in her, so that he shall have no need of spoil. She will do him good and not evil all the days of her life" (Prov. 31:11–12).

No matter how strong the commitment and attraction, problems related to companioning will arise. The problem-free relationship does not exist. Remember, the problems are not the real problem. No matter what situation people find themselves in, the number of problems are so great that they cannot be added up (Eccles. 1:15). Failure to deal biblically with problems is the real culprit. This failure may result in the destruction of the relationship. That's why Jesus said, "If thou bring thy gift to the altar, and there rememberest that thy brother hath aught against thee; leave there thy gift before the altar, and go thy way; first be reconciled to thy brother, and then come and offer thy gift" (Matt. 5:23–24). Commitment to dealing biblically with problems is essential if companioning is to be kept on a positive track.

The existence of problems in relationships requires the pair to constantly *adjust* to one another. Accommodating one's self to an ever-changing partner is both exciting and challenging. We must consistently seek to know where our partners are and what their needs are. These needs will change dramatically as the marriage goes through various stages, and each stage will present the couple with unique challenges.

At the same time we must know how to appropriately express our personal needs. The Shulamite maiden in the Song of Solomon provides an excellent example of a person who appropriately expresses a need. She says, "Thou that dwellest in the gardens, the companions hearken to thy voice: cause me to hear it. Make haste, my beloved, and be thou like to a roe or to a young hart upon the mountains of spices" (Song of Sol. 8:13–14).

The young lover has returned from his journey and is having a great time talking to his friends. She is sitting back waiting patiently for their time together. It's not happening. Should she wait dutifully and submissively? No; she is a person and their covenant has placed him under obligations to her. She asserts her right as his companion. This type of assertiveness is essential if solid companioning that has intimacy as its goal is to be achieved. She knows that and she speaks. She asks him to adjust and meet her needs.

Intimacy is possible only when persons know how to lovingly communicate their needs. *Argument* will sometimes follow such moments of sharing. These arguments are to be welcomed. They are like pains that precede the birth of something new and exciting. Paul and Barnabas argued over John Mark (Acts 15:37–40). Thank God, Barnabas asserted his right to differ with Paul. John Mark will be eternally grateful.

Many times over the course of our marriage Peg has argued with me. She has tolerated an area of failure or wrong in my life and finally spoken the truth. She has obeyed the biblical mandate to speak the truth in love (Eph. 4:15).

In the early years of my life I spent a lot of time in school. When I wasn't in school I was working at the church with young people. She was at home taking care of two young children. When I came home I was glued to the television set. I wasn't much help or encouragement to her. Finally, when she had taken all of my indifference to her needs she could, she confronted me. She said, in effect, "Cause me to hear your voice and give me a hand with our children."

My first response was retreat, but I couldn't stay away. The Holy Spirit convicted me through her words. I knew I needed to *cooperate* with the Holy Spirit and Peg for the production of change in my life. I needed to adjust. I needed to do things differently. I needed to be a real companion. It would be a sin for me to attempt to dominate her and merely meet my needs through our relationship. It would be a sin for me to offer her a series of rationalizations that allowed me to selfishly pursue my own ambition. I loved her and I wanted to be a good husband and a good companion. The desire to be a good companion was accompanied in me by the awareness that I needed to repent of my sins against her. Repentance for me meant acknowledging my areas of failure and seeking God's and Peg's forgiveness.

It is important to understand that the future direction of our relationship hinged on my willingness to repent. Other alternatives did flood my mind. I wanted, on the one hand, to justify my behavior. On the other hand, I knew I was sinning against our relationship. I am grateful for what happened in our relationship. I think the level of intimacy we have achieved would have been impossible without the conflict we experienced and the resolution of that conflict. I abandoned power. I might have locked into it and attempted to destroy her perceptions. Instead, I cooperated with the Holy Spirit, who replaced my will to rebel and control with the will to relate. Peg cooperated with the Holy Spirit and freely forgave me.

The will to relate would have had little value if it had not been accompanied by a desire to *edify* and serve my mate. Paul speaks of serving when he says, "Let nothing be done through strife or vainglory; but in lowliness of mind let each esteem other better than themselves. Look not every man on his own things, but every man also on the things of others" (Phil. 2:3–4). In these verses are the most vital issues for the continuation of companioning. Are we able to get hold of ourselves, see what sin is doing to destroy our relationships, rebuke ourselves, repent, and direct our energies away from selfish interests to meeting needs in our mates' lives? The practice of these behaviors will assure the ongoing development of a companioning that will make intimacy real in our relationships.

People can do these things, but not without the assistance of the Holy Spirit. I think Paul had areas like marital communication in mind when he said, "Work out your own salvation with fear and trembling" (Phil. 2:12). When I think of the tragic consequences of the negative companioning cycle, I am afraid. I don't think any couple is exempt from the forces that contribute to the beginning and continuation of such a negative cycle. We must join our wills to the power of God's Spirit to keep such cycles from dominating our relationships.

The Holy Spirit is ever ready to assist us with fulfilling the desire to edify our mates. We ought to seek to serve and edify from a position of knowledge (1 Peter 3:7). The goal is to participate with the Holy Spirit in the edification of our mates in specific concrete ways. Paul says, "Let us therefore follow after the things which make for peace, and things wherewith one may edify another" (Rom. 14:19).

Companioning demands a wholehearted commitment to strengthening mates. It takes two individuals for companioning to be a reality. Companioning can be interrupted at any time by self-centered forces that devalue or weaken the partner. Each individual must keep such forces from doing their terrible damage.

Principles for Building Intimacy Through Companioning

All spouses have experienced the consequences of negative companioning at one time or another in their marriages. All have felt the hurt of these negative forces and witnessed their power to interrupt and end relationships. What follows are suggested principles that should be understood and applied by couples who wish to strengthen intimacy through better companioning.

Good companioning involves our free choice of our partner as a companion and our unconditional acceptance of his or her unique personality.

Good companioning rests on the conviction that we are completely loved by our mate. We need change nothing to win or retain that love. Mates don't earn each other's love and cannot lose it.

Good companioning is a result of our attempt to understand the legitimate needs of our companion and the commitment of one's total resources to the meeting of those needs.

Good companioning requires a commitment to majoring on the positive while in the presence of the companion. The edification that results from such sharing should be the goal for our times together. We must schedule time to deal with negative "stuff" apart from those times when our conversation and interaction is focused on the positive.

Good companioning involves our free choice to spend the bulk of leisure time with the companion of choice. This does not mean we have no other friends and do nothing with others. However, it is clear to everyone that the majority of our leisure time is spent with our mates, who are our most important friends. Too much outside involvement violates the spirit of selective love that motivated us to enter into covenant with our companions. They plan "sharing days," "sharing trips," and "sharing moments" to enhance our intimacy.

Good companioning operates through good days and bad days. It is irrational to believe that any two people can have a relationship that is always "upbeat." We expect bad days and should give each other space at times. When we have caused a problem should be willing to say, "I'm sorry." Sometimes neither has caused the problem; bad days come because of outside pressures. When conflict arises, partners who value their friendship handle it as soon as possible. Rather than punish one another they make negotiation and compromise their primary objective. When one wins, both win; when one loses, both lose.

Good companioning results from our willingness to allow for and support individual differences. Good companions don't try to make each other over to fit some predetermined mold. Good companions allow for change in their partners. Change will come across the stages of life, and good companions plan to stay in touch so we can respond appropriately.

Good companioning involves a willingness to speak to a partner in a language of love that communicates. Some people receive love only when it is spoken, others when it is given in the form of gifts, others when it opens doors of opportunity, and others when it is accompanied by touch. Companioning is not possible if we cannot communicate our love for our mates in a language that is meaningful to them.

Good companions do not try to meet every need that partners have. We meet those we have the resources to meet. Only Jesus Christ can meet some of our mates needs. Friends, parents, and others will meet needs. Good companions recognize what they can do for their mates and gladly do it, but they also recognize their limitations.

Good companions tell each other the truth. The trust we have in one another provides a valuable foundation from which we are free to speak the truth in love.

Good companions are open and comfortable with one another. There is a sense of togetherness that causes us to constantly desire to exchange quality gifts with one another. What follows is a list of some of the quality gifts companions give to one another.

These gifts serve to strengthen the intimacy we enjoy. Good companions:

Spend time together. We give the gift of time.
Have fun together. We give the gift of laughter.
Share feelings and thoughts. We give the gift of sharing.
Like being together. We give the gift of appreciation.
Discuss issues. We give the gift of confidence.
Survive crises together. We give the gift of dependability.
Discuss fears. We give the gift of vulnerability.
Cover our partners' weaknesses. We give the gift of protection.
Celebrate our individual values together. We give the gift of respect.
Encourage a life separate from our life together. We give the gift of separateness.
Speak the truth together. We give the gift of honesty.
Handle conflict together. We give the gift of surfaced anger.
Practice forgiveness. We give the gift of forgiveness.
Practice unconditional acceptance. We give the gift of love.

Conclusion

Strengthening marital intimacy is a goal worth working for in marriages. Intimacy is only possible when two persons celebrate their oneness and their separateness. The stronger the individuals, the stronger the team when they are pledged to oneness.

Men sometimes forget that they bear a great responsibility for the type of atmosphere that exists in the home. Humble leadership that binds the family together with love and sponsors the growth of its individuals should be our goal. Women need to do all they can to produce a loving atmosphere so that the force of the male contribution will not be deminished.

Growth Exercises

The following assignment is designed to help you improve the quality of companioning you are experiencing as a couple. Both husband and wife should answer each item.

Name your three best friends.

What is it about these people that has contributed most to building your friendship?

What are the three things that you most need from your husband or wife?

At present how is your husband or wife meeting the three needs you listed above?

In your opinion, how could the needs you listed above be more fully met by your mate?

We spoke of the language of love that really communicates. When you seek to show your love for your mate, do you:

> Say it with words
> Say it with touch
> Say it with opportunity
> Say it with help
> Say it with things
> Say it with _____

Ask your mate if you are speaking his or her language effectively.

What are some needs your mate has that you think you cannot meet?

List some things you enjoy doing as a couple. Try to mention at least five.

Give an example of something the two of you did together that you could never have done without your partner's help.

Check the things in the following list that you think best buddies would do if they had an argument.

> Give up on each other.
> Try to resolve the problem if at all possible.
> Place all the blame on the other person.
> Get another friend right away to replace the old one.
> Forgive each other.
> Tell everybody how awful the other person is.
> Pray for the alienated friend.
> Try to get a neutral friend to arbitrate the differences.
> Seek to really understand
>   where the other person is coming from.
> Hear the other person out.

Now go back and star (*) the things you do when you have an argument with your husband or wife.

How do you show your mate that you are grateful for the contribution he or she makes in your life?

Give an example of a time when you told your mate the truth in love. How did he or she receive what you said? What did you do then?

What are some things about your friend (mate) that you are willing to just let ride?

What follows is a list of ways to assure that you and your partner get quality time together. Check the ones you practice. Star the ones you think you might like to start doing.

> Schedule trips together.
> Schedule a night of the week that is yours together.
> Schedule breakfast once a week together.
> Schedule walks together.
> Schedule time to pray together.
> Schedule time to shop together.
> Schedule time to work around the house together.
> Schedule time to play together.
> Schedule time to visit friends together.
> Schedule time to plan.
> Schedule time to look at finances.
> Schedule time to share ideas.

I know some of you are getting worried about the word *schedule,* but what you do not schedule, frequently gets crowded out by all the other things that are important for you to do.

Go back to the list of quality gifts that companions give to one another. The list contains fourteen gifts. Each of you now make this covenant with God concerning your partner: "For the next fourteen weeks I will make it a point to give, at the very least, one of these special gifts to my mate each week." One way to implement this covenant is to write these gifts son slips of paper and put them in a bowl. Each Sunday night before you go to bed, draw one of the slips from the bowl and ask God to help you give that gift to your companion in the week ahead.

Additional Reading

Patricia Gundry. *Heirs Together.* Grand Rapids: Zondervan, 1980.

Charles M. Sell. *Achieving the Impossible: Intimate Marriage.* Portland, Ore.: Multnomah, 1982.

Edward Wheat. *Love Life.* Grand Rapids: Zondervan, 1980.